CONTENTS

PLANNING YOUR REMODELING PROJECT

Almost every home can benefit from a little remodeling. Newer houses, for instance, often have basement space that could be divided into several rooms to provide for separate activities and more efficient storage. Small, warrenlike rooms in older homes can be transformed into larger, more inviting spaces by rearranging or removing a wall or two. In addition, by remodeling you can adapt a home to meet the changing needs of your family or to correct design problems produced by poor planning or construction in the past.

For the most part, an interior remodeling project involves demolition and construction of walls and ceilings made with dimension lumber and drywall or plaster surfaces. As a do-it-yourselfer,

you'll need only basic carpentry skills for framing new walls and covering them with drywall and some finish carpentry techniques for installing trim.

What's in this book

The first three chapters present general information for anyone contemplating a remodeling project. They include advice on planning the job, the tools and materials you'll need, and basic building techniques. The second part of the book covers the specifics of remodeling: demolition, framing walls, installing and finishing drywall, installing a dropped ceiling, repairing wall surfaces, and installing doors and trim.

Each of the projects in this book begins with a Prestart Checklist that gives you a

clear idea of the tools, materials, and skills involved, as well as how long it will take. The step-by-step directions on the top half of each page lead you through each project. On the bottom half, Stanley Pro Tips provide added advice and information to help you work easier and smarter. "What if …" boxes help you deal with unusual situations.

Getting started

In this chapter you'll learn how to translate your remodeling needs and desires into a program, and then focus that program into floor plans and materials lists. Enjoy the planning process. The results may surprise, but always should please, starting your project on a path to success.

For all but the simplest remodeling projects, a good plan is essential for success.

CHAPTER PREVIEW

Anatomy of walls and ceilings
page 6

Developing a project plan
page 8

Is this wall structural?
page 10

What's in the wall?
page 11

Interior
Walls
FRAMING, DRYWALLING, TRIMMING

Meredith® Books
Des Moines, Iowa

Stanley® Books
An imprint of Meredith® Books

Stanley Interior Walls
Editor: Ken Sidey
Senior Associate Design Director: Tom Wegner
Assistant Editor: Harijs Priekulis
Copy Chief: Terri Fredrickson
Copy and Production Editor: Victoria Forlini
Editorial Operations Manager: Karen Schirm
Managers, Book Production: Pam Kvitne,
    Marjorie J. Schenkelberg
Contributing Copy Editor: Kim Catanzarite
Technical Editor, The Stanley Works: Mike Maznio
Contributing Proofreaders: Sue Fetters, Kathy Roth Eastman,
    Ellie Sweeney
Technical Reviewer: Tom Garcia
Contributing Illustrator: Dave Brandon
Contributing Photographer: Scott Little
Electronic Production Coordinator: Paula Forest
Editorial and Design Assistants: Renee E. McAtee,
    Karen McFadden

Additional Editorial Contributions from
    Nailhaus Publications, Inc.
Publishing Director: David Schiff
Writer: Kenneth S. Burton Jr.
Administrative Assistant: Aliza K. Schiff

Photography from
    Image Studios
Account Executive: Lisa Egan
Photography: Bill Rein
Set Building: Rick Nadke

Meredith® Books
Publisher and Editor in Chief: James D. Blume
Design Director: Matt Strelecki
Managing Editor: Gregory H. Kayko
Executive Editor, Gardening and Home Improvement:
    Benjamin W. Allen
Executive Editor, Home Improvement: Larry Erickson

Director, Operations: George A. Susral
Director, Production: Douglas M. Johnston
Executive Director, Sales: Ken Zagor

Vice President and General Manager: Douglas J. Guendel

Meredith Publishing Group
President, Publishing Group: Stephen M. Lacy
Vice President-Publishing Director: Bob Mate

Meredith Corporation
Chairman and Chief Executive Officer: William T. Kerr

Chairman of the Executive Committee: E.T. Meredith III

All of us at Stanley® Books are dedicated to providing you with the information and ideas you need to enhance your home and garden. We welcome your comments and suggestions about this book. Write to us at:
    Meredith Corporation
    Stanley Books
    1716 Locust St.
    Des Moines, IA 50309–3023

If you would like more information on other Stanley products, call 1-800-STANLEY or visit us at: www.stanleyworks.com Stanley® and the notched rectangle around the Stanley name are registered trademarks of The Stanley Works and subsidiaries.

If you would like to purchase any of our home improvement, cooking, crafts, gardening, or home decorating and design books, check wherever quality books are sold. Or visit us at: meredithbooks.com

Note to the Readers: Due to differing conditions, tools, and individual skills, Meredith Corporation assumes no responsibility for any damages, injuries suffered, or losses incurred as a result of following the information published in this book. Before beginning any project, review the instructions carefully, and if any doubts or questions remain, consult local experts or authorities. Because codes and regulations vary greatly, you always should check with authorities to ensure that your project complies with all applicable local codes and regulations. Always read and observe all of the safety precautions provided by manufacturers of any tools, equipment, or supplies, and follow all accepted safety procedures.

The planning stage of a remodeling project takes time, but it's time well spent. A good plan helps focus your dreams into a manageable reality and helps prevent costly mistakes.

ANATOMY OF WALLS AND CEILINGS

The projects featured in this book revolve around the construction and modification of interior walls and spaces. They involve basic carpentry skills and techniques. Most houses in this country are stick framed; that is, their skeletons are built from a framework of relatively small pieces of wood. Typically walls are framed with 2×4s. This makes walls about 4½-inches thick (3½ inches of wood covered on both sides by ½-inch-thick drywall.) The illustration on the opposite page shows how the assembled pieces form a wall and names the specific parts of the framing.

Terminology

All 2×4s look the same, but as you begin to fasten them together, you'll call them different names depending on their position within the wall. The **studs** are the vertical pieces that make up most of a wall's frame. The cavities in between the studs are called **bays** (or stud bays). A horizontal piece at the bottom of the wall is called the **bottom plate.** The studs are nailed to the plate, which in turn is nailed to the floor. At the top of the wall is the **top plate.** Often a doubled 2×4,

it anchors the top ends of the studs as well as ties the wall into the ceiling.

In new construction, the walls are usually built flat on the floor with a single top plate. The second layer, which ties them together, is added after the walls are raised into position. Sometimes **blocking** is added between the studs. Blocking provides a solid spot in the wall for attaching things such as cabinets or handrails. In some situations, blocking is required as a firestop where a stud bay extends between floors. This keeps the bay from acting as a chimney for a fire. Without firestops, a fire could quickly spread from floor to floor. Blocking and extra studs are also used to catch the edge of the drywall at corners and in places where the stud spacing doesn't work out perfectly.

Openings for doors or windows

An opening in a wall, such as one for a doorway or window, has its own set of terms. The opening itself is called the **rough opening.** The size of the rough opening is specified by the manufacturer of the door or window. Typically it's 1 inch larger than the outside dimensions of whatever is to fill it. Doubled studs stand on both sides of the

opening. One stud of each pair runs from plate to plate; this is the **king stud.** The other stud determines the height of the opening. This is the **jack stud** or **trimmer.** Resting on top of the jack stud is a **header.** Depending on how much weight (load) the wall has to carry, the header may be fairly thick (the weight has to be transferred from over the opening to the jack studs) or it may be quite thin (if the wall doesn't support any weight). Sometimes headers are topped by short pieces of wood known as **cripple studs,** which are used to help support drywall and trim pieces.

Types of walls

A wall that supports the weight of the building above is a **bearing wall** and is said to be **structural** *(page 10).* If a wall merely divides the interior space, it is not structural but simply a **partition wall.**

The framing members in the floor and in the ceiling are called **joists.** Underfoot, a **subfloor** is nailed to the joists. The walls are usually fastened to the subfloor. Overhead, drywall can be attached to the underside of the ceiling joists, or if you prefer the grid for a dropped ceiling can be attached to them.

FRAMED WITH 2×4S
Skip the skinny sticks

You might be tempted to frame a wall using 2×3s to save a little money and space, but don't do it. The slight amount of space you'll gain and the few pennies you'll save are not worth the frustration you'll encounter working with 2×3s. These skinny sticks of lumber are notorious for warping and twisting. If you start building with warped and twisted wood, there is little chance that the wall will turn out straight and true.

Why 16 inches?

In much residential construction, the wall studs and the floor and ceiling joists are spaced 16 inches on center. ("On center" or "OC" indicates the distance from the center of one piece to the center of the next.) Why 16 inches? Plywood or oriented strand board used to sheathe the outside of the walls and the drywall used to finish the inside all come in sheets 48 inches wide. The number 48 is evenly divisible by 16. Spacing studs and joists 16 inches on center is a nice compromise between adequate support and economy, while still allowing efficient use of 4×8 sheet stock.

FRAMING TERMINOLOGY

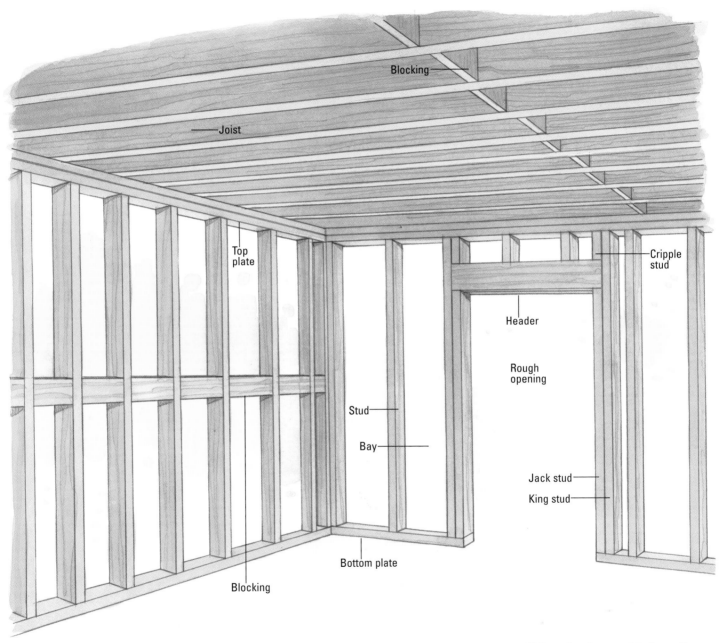

Before planning your interior wall project, learn the names and roles of all the wall-framing components.

DEVELOPING A PROJECT PLAN

Remodeling a house, or even just a room within a house, disrupts daily home life and requires hard work and money, making it well worth the time it takes to plan the project before you begin. A good plan reveals problems before they happen and suggests solutions that might not have occurred to you otherwise.

The first part of developing a remodeling plan is to put together a program. A program is a list of the results you would like to accomplish by remodeling. Try to be as objective as you can when working on the program. If you start out listing "more closet space," you are likely to be locked into developing a plan for closets.

If, however, you list "more storage space," you may discover a better, more workable solution than an additional closet provides.

Once you have your program, draw a floor plan of the existing space and make copies of it using tracing paper overlays. Sketch in ideas that accomplish the goals defined in your program. Draw each idea on a different copy of the floor plan to compare or combine them.

1 Start by drawing a floor plan of the existing space on graph paper. Most of the time, a scale of ¼ inch to 1 foot allows plenty of detail without being so big that you need a large piece of paper. Show all the walls, doorways, and windows.

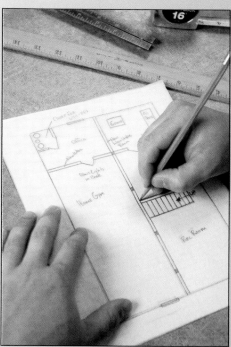

2 Once you have completed your floor plan, make tracing paper overlays to test out possible designs. Avoid erasing—if you make a mistake or if you don't like the way something looks, just make another overlay.

Create a clear materials list

As you go over your drawings to list the materials you need, a couple of steps make the task easier. First, divide the list into four parts: **lumber** (for 2× material), **trim** (for moldings and 1× material), **sheet stock** (for drywall and plywood), and **miscellaneous** (for fasteners, hardware, doors, and such).

Second, be consistent in the way you list the sizes of the lumber needed. List it as thickness × width × length. Don't worry about adding in the units of measure (feet and inches). For example, a 2×4×8 is an 8-foot 2×4.

When to involve the building inspector

Almost every community has some kind of building code: a set of rules that spell out who can build what in a house, and what standards a construction job must meet. While the requirements can seem a nuisance, building codes are worthwhile—they protect everyone from shoddy work and potentially dangerous construction practices.

Rules vary from community to community. In some areas, for example, anyone can do electrical wiring, as long as it is inspected. In other areas, inspections are only required for jobs costing more than a certain amount. Some areas allow you to do your own work; others require a licensed electrician

To stay on the right side of the law, the best thing to do is to call your local zoning or code enforcement office. Find out exactly what is allowed in your community and what you

must do to comply. You may even want to set up an appointment to talk with a building inspector about your project.

If you do meet with an inspector, make up a list of questions to ask ahead of time. While most inspectors are happy to point you in the right direction, they are busy and will appreciate it if you have thought out what you need to know ahead of time. Key questions to ask are:

■ Do I need a permit to build the project I have in mind?

■ What information will I need to provide to apply for the permit?

■ If I need to supply drawings, do they need to be signed by an engineer or architect?

■ What inspections will I need?

■ How do I arrange for an inspection?

■ Is there anything I am forgetting to ask?

3 When you are happy with your new floor plan, make a scale elevation of the new design. An elevation is a view of a wall's face. The same ¼-inch-to-1-foot scale works well here.

4 Create an overlay for the elevation drawing. On it show the framing that you will be doing and include the critical dimensions of the new design. If there are problems or special circumstances, note them in the margins.

5 Use your framing diagram to make up a materials list. Keep in mind the bottom plate of a wall runs the length of the wall even if you plan to include doors. You'll cut the part that runs across the doorway after the wall is in place.

Thinking about light and traffic

Any time you build new walls, whether to divide an open basement into rooms or to rearrange other living spaces, you alter the dynamic within your home. Some changes are obvious— you now have an office instead of a desk tucked away in a corner. Others are much subtler— the basement is now a lot darker because the only window is in the new office.

Subtle changes can be tough to predict, and therefore, hard to plan around. But there are two that you specifically need to consider: how your alterations will affect the light in the space and how they will affect traffic flow.

As you plan, sit in the space at different times of the day and note how light enters the room. Perhaps your plan to divide a room allows plenty of windows in both new spaces, but are you blocking morning sun from the new breakfast nook? What can you do to keep the alteration from having a negative impact on the space?

Can you add interior windows or a half-wall partition that lets the light continue to penetrate deeply into the space? Filling the top half of the wall with glass blocks is an effective way to create privacy without blocking light.

Traffic is the other issue that deserves serious consideration. Will your proposed change redirect traffic through your house? Will the kitchen suddenly become the preferred thoroughfare to the back door? It may be worth marking off the proposed spaces with tape, or even cardboard, to try out various arrangements before settling on the final plan.

Adding a wall in the basement can stop sunlight from reaching into the room. A door with glass panels may be the solution.

IS THIS WALL STRUCTURAL?

As you plan a remodeling job, you'll begin to see your house in a new light. Things that appeared permanent before—walls, for example—may not seem that way anymore. You will soon realize that almost any alteration is possible, if you are willing to do the work and bear the expense. Before you get carried away and start knocking down walls, however, you need to understand that there are two kinds of walls in a house: bearing and nonbearing (or partition) walls.

Bearing walls help carry the weight of the building and its contents to the ground. **Partition walls** simply divide up the space. It is far easier to remove or relocate a partition wall than it is to do the same to a bearing wall. In many cases you may want to rethink your project before deciding to remove or modify a bearing wall.

How to spot the difference

The next step in planning is to determine whether an interior wall is a bearing wall. This book deals only with interior remodeling, so discussion is limited to interior walls.

If the wall runs parallel to the ceiling and floor joists, it is probably not a bearing wall. Short closet walls, for example, usually are not bearing. If the wall runs perpendicular to the ceiling and floor joists, there is a good chance that it is a bearing wall

How can you tell which way the joists run? Most of the time joists run perpendicular to the roof's ridgeline. If the wall is under an attic, go up there and see if the joists cross over the wall. If joists end on top of a wall, you know for sure it's a bearing wall. If the attic has floorboards, they run across the

joists, and you'll see the lines of nails where they are fastened to the joists. If your roof is supported by trusses, the answer is simpler. Trusses have diagonal pieces that run from the attic floor to ceiling. They transfer the weight of the roof only to the outside walls, so all the interior walls in the story directly below are probably partition walls.

If you can't check above, check below. Is there a wall directly under the one you want to remove or modify? If there is, they are probably both bearing walls. If there is a basement or crawlspace below the wall you want to change, go there and see if a beam supported by posts or piers is directly under the wall. If so, you can assume the wall above is bearing.

If you still have doubts, hire a carpenter or a structural engineer to help you.

IDENTIFYING A BEARING WALL

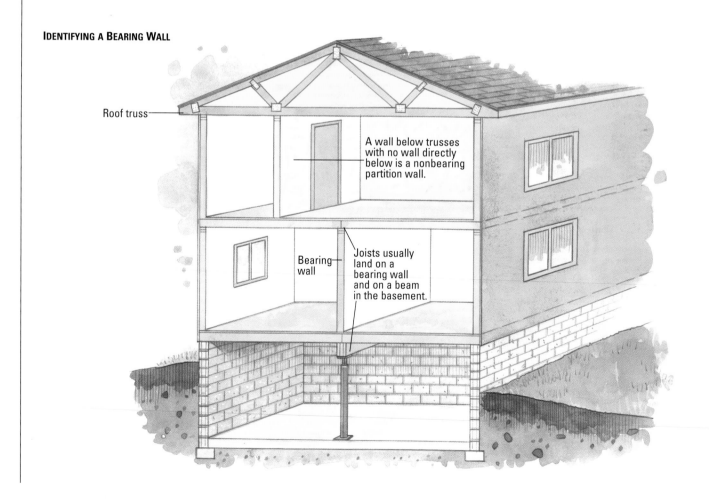

Roof truss

A wall below trusses with no wall directly below is a nonbearing partition wall.

Bearing wall

Joists usually land on a bearing wall and on a beam in the basement.

WHAT'S IN THE WALL?

When you start thinking about modifying existing walls, you need to consider what runs through their bays. The walls in most houses are strung with a network of wires, pipes, and ductwork for the various utility systems. If you decide to move or get rid of a wall, you must deal with the utilities it contains.

At the very least, a wall contains some electrical wiring. You'll see evidence of it on the surface in the form of receptacles or switches. Wiring is easier to reroute than other utility systems.

As for plumbing and ductwork, the best way to determine if the wall contains one or the other is to get underneath the house in a basement or crawlspace and see what goes up into the wall. These utilities seldom run horizontally through a wall, so if you don't see anything running up into the wall from underneath, there's probably no plumbing or ductwork in the wall. Note likely utility locations on your plan.

Once you have an idea of what you are up against, call the appropriate trade professionals and explain the situation to them. Tell them what you are doing and ask at what point they want to come and remove, reroute, or add to the system. Most will want you to notify them when the wall is stripped of its covering, so they can come in and get right to work.

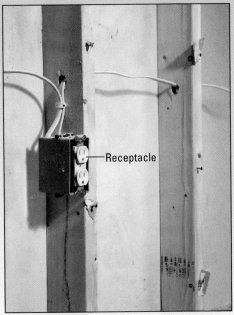

Electrical wiring is found in most walls. Most receptacles are wired in conjunction with receptacles on other walls, so changing the wiring may be more involved than it first appears. Check both sides of a wall and neighboring walls.

Receptacle

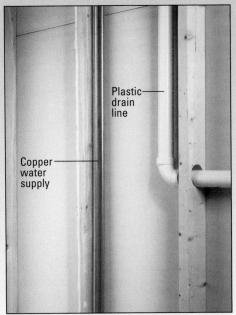

Plastic drain line

Copper water supply

Plumbing also can be part of a wall modification. If there is a bathroom or kitchen directly above (and sometimes below) the wall you intend to work on, you will probably find pipes in that wall.

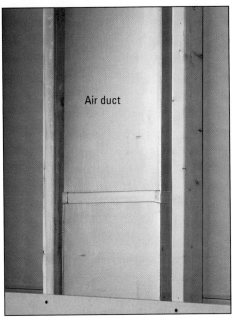

Air duct

Heating and air-conditioning ductwork is difficult to trace. Often second floor vent lines and return air lines pass through stud bays but are difficult to spot from underneath because other ducts block them from view.

Drain line

Drain-waste-vent lines can be trickier to locate than plumbing supply lines; they take less direct routes. Besides being much larger than supply lines, drain lines often run from the basement through the roof, requiring extensive work to reroute.

STANLEY PRO TIP

Schedule the pros

If you discover something in a wall that you don't want to move or remove yourself, you'll need to hire a professional to do the job. If you do hire a plumber; electrician; or a heating, ventilation, and air-conditioning contractor, be sure to schedule his or her time before you start demolition. Keep in mind, the tradesperson may have to come twice: once to disconnect and again to reconnect after you frame the new walls.

CHOOSING TOOLS

As you walk through the tool aisles of any well-stocked home center or hardware store, the choices will seem overwhelming. The following pointers will help you purchase the best tools for your purposes without spending more money than necessary.

Rule No. 1: Never buy a tool before you need it. Purchasing a tool because you think you might need it someday destines that tool to years of collecting dust.

When you decide you need a hand tool, purchase the best quality you can afford, especially when it comes to edge tools, such as chisels and planes. Any chisel or plane will last a lifetime, but lower-cost, lower-quality tools cost you in time, convenience, and precision—cheap chisels don't stay sharp, and cheap planes don't cut flat and don't adjust smoothly. The metal on all hand tools should be flawlessly machined, and handles should be tight-fitting, hefty, and comfortable.

Power tools

When it comes to power tools, the shopping strategy is a little different. Consider if you need to buy the tool at all. If, for example, you don't expect to do much trim work after you remodel the den, consider renting a power miter box instead of buying one.

If you do decide to purchase a power tool, you probably don't need the top-of-the-line contractor's model. These tools are worth the money to pros who use them all day, every day. For your purposes, a lighter-duty saber saw will do a fine job, for example, of notching wainscot boards around electrical boxes.

While you don't need the most heavy-duty power tools, you do want tools that are well-made. Check that cast-steel parts are smoothly milled. Look for knobs that are hefty enough to tighten and loosen easily—stamped steel wing nuts are a sign of a cheap tool. Inevitably you will dangle a power tool by its cord as you lower it from a ladder to the ground, so make sure the cord is sturdy and reinforced where it enters the housing.

Be aware that the horsepower rating of a tool means little; amperage rating is the true measure of power. Finally, pick up the tool and make sure it feels comfortable in your hands.

Start out with the best-quality hand tools you can afford—they pay off in the long run.

CHAPTER PREVIEW

Measuring and layout tools
page 14

Demolition and construction tools
page 16

Power cutting tools
page 18

Drilling and shaping tools
page 21

Protect cutting tools from damage by storing them with their cutting edges covered.

Invest in comfortable safety equipment, including ear protection and eyewear, and make a habit of using it.

Finishing tools
page 23

Accessories
page 24

Renting
page 25

Carpentry and remodeling involve a variety of tools and supplies. To protect your investment, store tools in toolboxes when they are not in use. Keep like tools together in separate carriers so they are easier to find when needed.

MEASURING AND LAYOUT TOOLS

As you assemble a collection of tools for remodeling work, remember that you don't have to purchase everything at once. Start by purchasing only those tools you need for the job at hand, then add to your collection as the scope of your work expands. As a do-it-yourselfer, you probably do not need the top-of-the-line, most expensive models. But buying good-quality tools from the start ensures many years of service from your purchase.

Tools for measuring

Carpenters live by three rules: plumb (pieces are vertically straight), square (pieces are 90 degrees perpendicular), and level (pieces are horizontally straight). The need for these rules starts from the ground up. A foundation that isn't level and square inevitably leads to trouble throughout a house as construction progresses. Learn to adhere to these standards, and your work

will look professional and create fewer problems as you go.

Working on an older home, however, teaches you that plumb, square, and level are ideals and often not realities. In an older building, you may have to compromise between what is right and what looks right. The two are often quite different.

The tools shown here come in handy as you plan, lay out, and build. A **tape measure**

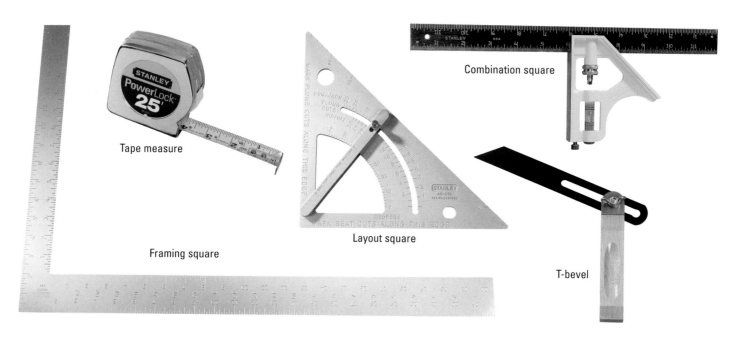

Tape measure

Framing square

Layout square

Combination square

T-bevel

Checking a square for square

1 A framing square that is truly square is a valuable tool; one that is almost square is next to worthless. To check the accuracy of a framing square, hold the square along the edge of a straight board and draw a line.

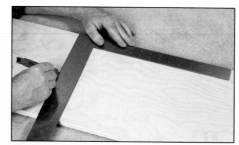

2 Flip over the square and draw a second line right over the first. If the lines coincide, the square is square.

3 You can adjust a framing square by striking it with a center punch and hammer. Punch the square near the outside corner to close the angle. Punch it near the inside corner (as shown above) to open it up.

provides a compact ruler for all measuring tasks. A 25-foot model is the most common, although a 16-footer proves adequate for most jobs. A **combination square** allows you to draw square lines across boards for crosscutting. It is also handy for making layout lines a specific distance in from the edge of a board. A **layout square** does many of the same tasks and serves as a circular saw fence when crosscutting. A **framing square** (also called a carpenter's square) can be used for larger layouts. A **T-bevel** transfers angles from one place to another.

To check for level, you'll need a good **level** or two. They come in many lengths; a 3- or 4-foot model is a good first purchase. A **plumb bob** is simply a heavy, pointed weight. When dangled from a string, a plumb bob and the string provide a vertical reference. A **chalk line** is used to mark long, straight lines. Many chalk lines also serve as plumb bobs. A **stud finder** is used to find framing studs behind walls. Electronic and magnetic finders detect the nails in a wall but can be fooled by wires and pipes. New models use sound to sense the density of the studs.

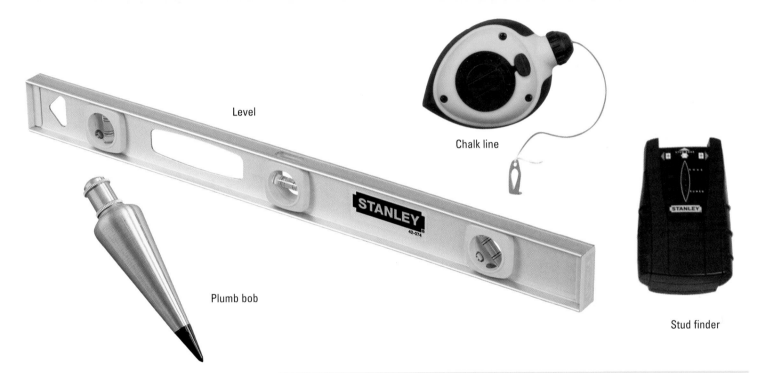

Level

Chalk line

Plumb bob

Stud finder

Using a tape

The hook on the end of a tape measure is loose for a reason. When taking an inside measurement, it slips up tight to the end of the tape, its thickness becoming part of the measurement. When hooked over the end of a board, it slides out to compensate for the missing thickness.

STANLEY PRO TIP: **Use chalk lines for long, straight marks**

Snapping a line: Mark the ends of the line. Hook the chalk line at one mark, stretch it taut, and hold it at the other mark. Lift straight up and pluck the line to make your mark.

Chalk for chalked lines comes in a variety of colors. For marking complex layouts, use two or more lines, each with its own color.

DEMOLITION AND CONSTRUCTION TOOLS

You probably already have some basic carpentry tools around the house. To handle the demands of a remodeling project, make sure the tools you have are good quality and in good condition. If not, purchase new ones.

One of the most basic tools is the hammer. A **16-ounce framing hammer** is an essential. It is heavy enough to drive the large nails used for framing, yet small enough for use when installing moldings. Add a **22-ounce framing hammer** for heavy work. **Straight and phillips screwdrivers** are necessary for installing hardware and occasionally for opening a paint can. A **utility knife** does everything from sharpening your pencil to cutting drywall. Keep plenty of blades on hand and replace them often so you always have a sharp cutting edge ready.

You'll find **nail sets** handy for driving finishing nails below the surface of moldings and extending your reach into hard-to-hammer places. An **awl** is a sharp pointed tool you'll use for marking hole locations and starting screws. For cutting and pulling small nails, nothing beats a set of **end nips.** Along the same line, three tools will handle

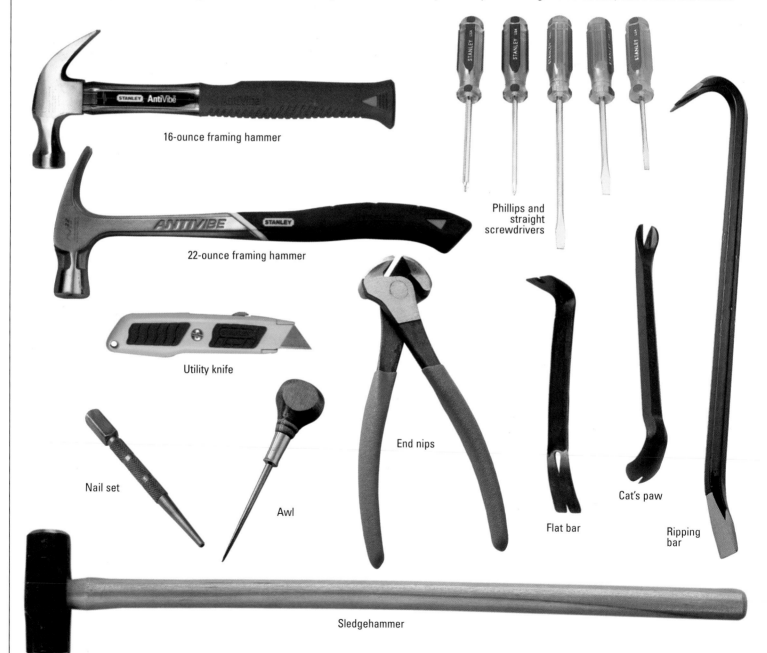

16-ounce framing hammer

22-ounce framing hammer

Phillips and straight screwdrivers

Utility knife

End nips

Nail set

Awl

Flat bar

Cat's paw

Ripping bar

Sledgehammer

your prying tasks: a **cat's paw** for pulling big nails, a **flat bar** for general prying, and a **ripping bar** for heavy-duty demolition. A **sledgehammer** is also useful for demolition and for nudging reluctant walls into position.

For cutting wood, you'll need some chisels, saws, and other edge tools. A **toolbox saw** packs a lot of cutting capability into a compact size. A **coping saw** is indispensable for cutting moldings at inside corners. For making accurate crosscuts and miters in molding, you'll need either a **miter box** or a power miter saw. For paring and fine-tuning the fit of door hinges and other hardware, you'll want a set of **chisels** (¼ inch, ½ inch, ¾ inch, and 1 inch). A **block plane** makes short work of trimming a door to size. A **putty knife** is another multipurpose tool. Its obvious use is for applying putty to fill nail holes, but it is also useful for prying off moldings without damage. Finally a pair of heavy-duty **metal snips** come in handy for a variety of cutting tasks, including the installation of metal studs.

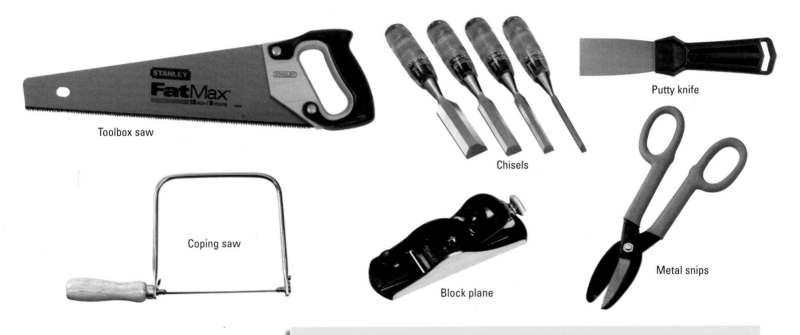

Toolbox saw

Chisels

Putty knife

Coping saw

Block plane

Metal snips

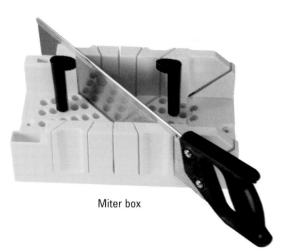

Miter box

STANLEY PRO TIP: **Keep cutting tools sharp**

1 For best results, keep your cutting tools sharp. Use a sharpening stone and honing oil. Drip some oil on the stone, then polish the tool's bevel, moving it in a figure-eight pattern. Make sure both the heel and toe of the bevel remain in contact with the stone.

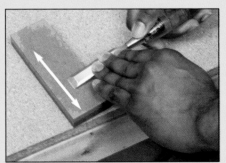

2 When all marks and other nicks are gone from the bevel, turn over the blade and polish the back. The combination of the two polished surfaces at the proper angle makes a sharp edge. Look at the edge in a strong light—a dull edge appears as a white line.

POWER CUTTING TOOLS

There are four types of power saws that will accomplish almost everything you'll need to do. The most useful is a <u>circular saw.</u> It will crosscut lumber and plywood to the right size, making straight cuts with ease. The most common saw uses a blade with a diameter of 7¼ inches. Most come with a steel-tipped combination blade, adequate for all the projects in this book. Steel blades dull quickly, though, so purchase a more durable carbide-tipped combination blade as a replacement. If you buy only one power saw, this is the one to get.

A **jigsaw** (sometimes called a saber saw) also crosscuts and rips lumber, though not as fast as a circular saw. Its chief characteristic is its ability to cut curves. Some models feature variable speed control, which is handy for cutting materials other than wood, such as plastic or metal. Some saber saws feature orbital cutting; the blade moves forward and back in addition to up and down, making the saw cut much faster than one without orbital action.

A **reciprocating saw** is handy for demolition work. It utilizes a variety of blades with teeth designed to cut different materials, including wood, nails, screws, and even steel pipes. Its blade can reach into tight places to make a cut, such as between framing members.

A **power miter saw,** also called a chop saw, is a stationary circular saw. While it makes clean crosscuts, its greatest strength is in making accurate miter (angled) cuts. If you have a lot of trim pieces to cut and install, a chop saw is the tool to use.

Circular saw

Jigsaw

Reciprocating saw

Power miter saw

CIRCULAR SAW
Buying one that's right for you

There are dozens of models of circular saws on the market. Here are some tips for selecting the one that's right for you:

First, you probably don't need a worm-drive saw. These heavy, relatively expensive tools are designed to withstand all-day framing jobs. They feature a worm gear that places the motor behind the shaft that drives the blade. This makes it easy to see where the blade is cutting but awkward for novices to use. Instead look for a good-quality "sidewinder," so named because the motor shaft is aligned beside the

blade and drives the blade directly. Sidewinders are much lighter and easier to handle than worm-drive saws. Various models have the blade on either side; find the model most comfortable to you. A good one will easily handle any project in this book.

Second, don't concern yourself with a saw's horsepower rating, which is usually measured when the saw is not under load. A better indication of a saw's power is its amperage rating. The cheapest saws are rated at 9 or 10 amps; find a saw rated at least 12 or 13 amps.

The saw should have a solid extruded or cast base, rather than a stamped-steel base. Check that the tilt and height adjustments work smoothly and tighten easily and firmly. Cast wing nuts stay tight more easily than the stamped wing nuts on cheaper saws. Levers work even better.

Finally make sure the saw is comfortable to use. If you can try different saws at the store, make some test cuts. Make sure you like the grip and the position of the switch and safety guard lever.

Using a circular saw

Crosscutting: To make a crosscut with a circular saw, draw a line across the piece, then cut on the waste side of the line. Support the piece so the waste falls freely away from the blade. The wider part of the saw's base (or shoe) rides on the part of the board that is supported.

Guided crosscutting: If you need a particularly precise cut, use a layout square as a guide. Line up the blade with the cut at the edge of the board. Then hold the square across the board with one edge against the side of the saw base. Push the saw along the square to make the cut.

Cutting plywood: Mark your layout lines with a chalk line. Support both sides of the cut with a series of 2×4s on a pair of sawhorses. Clamp a straightedge or board on the piece as a guide for the bottom plate of the circular saw. Set the saw to cut slightly deeper than the plywood thickness.

SAFETY FIRST
Preventing accidents and injuries

The importance of safety for home improvement and remodeling projects cannot be overemphasized. Mistakes can have serious consequences. Before starting any project, review all the steps involved. If you are uncomfortable with any procedure, find a carpenter or other knowledgeable person to help you.

Safety equipment should be among the first tools you purchase. Start with a pair of **safety glasses** or **goggles.** If you wear prescription glasses, get goggles that fit over them or invest in a pair of prescription safety glasses. Try them on before purchasing, and find a pair that is comfortable so

you won't mind wearing them whenever you're working. Make a habit of wearing safety glasses all the time, period. That way you won't be tempted to make "just one quick cut" without them.

Next up is hearing protection. There are many types of **earplugs** and **earmuffs** available. Earmuffs provide more complete protection. Again, try them on if possible to test for comfort.

Dust masks are necessary during demolition and drywall finishing. Check the label before you buy and match the mask to the type of work you are doing. In general, masks with a single strap are rated for nuisance dust.

These keep sawdust out of your lungs. For sanding drywall or ripping out plaster, you'll want a mask rated for fine dust. These thicker masks usually have two straps.

Protect your hands with **work gloves** when handling work such as unloading materials, demolition, and cleaning up debris. Do not wear them when you are working with power tools. You are more likely to lose your grip or fumble a tool or piece with gloves on. In addition, gloves may get caught in a spinning blade or drill bit.

Finally it is always a good idea to have a **first aid kit** on hand.

Safety goggles

Earmuffs

Safety glasses

Earplugs

Work gloves

Dust masks

First aid kit

There are two basic types of cuts to make using a circular saw: a cross cut, which runs across the grain; and a rip cut, which runs with the grain. No matter what type of cut you're making, for best results it should be straight.

The simple homemade cutting guide shown here helps you produce straight, accurate cuts with your circular saw. It is made from a piece of ¼-inch plywood and a straight length of ½-inch-thick stock. You can make the guide any length you like, up to 8 feet long for cutting sheets of plywood.

Making your own cutting guide

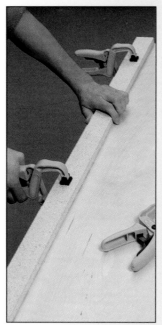  

1 Start with a piece of ¼-inch plywood that is at least 2½ inches wider than the base of your circular saw. Glue and screw a 2-inch-wide strip of ½-inch-thick stock flush to the long edge of the plywood.

2 Clamp the guide to a pair of sawhorses or on a bench. Place the saw base against the ½-inch stock and run the saw down the plywood, cutting it to the width. Make sure the blade won't cut the bench or horses.

3 To use the guide, clamp it to your workpiece with the sawed edge along a marked cut line. Guide the saw along the ½-inch stock to make the cut.

RIP CUTS
Cutting the long way

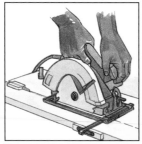

If you need to rip-cut boards, (for example, to make 4-inch-wide baseboards from 1×6s), use a rip guide accessory available for all circular saws. To make the cut, clamp the board securely across two sawhorses. Set the guide to the required width. Keep the guide firmly against the board.

SAFETY FIRST
Setting the correct depth of cut

When cutting with a circular saw, set the depth of cut so the blade extends through the material plus the depth of the teeth. This keeps the amount of exposed blade to a minimum while allowing the blade to cut efficiently. If the teeth reach just barely through the material, the blade may heat excessively and bind in the cut. As you are sawing, remember that the teeth reach past the underside of the board. Keep fingers, power cords, and other materials clear.

DRILLING AND SHAPING TOOLS

Along with power saws, you also will need a power drill or two and an assortment of bits and cutters for making holes. The tool to start with is a corded variable-speed, reversible **(VSR) drill,** with a ⅜-inch-diameter chuck. This tool handles 90 percent of your drilling needs. Along with the drill, purchase a set of **twist drill bits,** used for boring things such as pilot holes for screws. For larger holes, a set of **spade bits** does the trick. For really large holes, such as those for a lockset in a door, use a **hole saw,** which fits into a drill.

The next drill to acquire is a **cordless drill/driver,** which comes in a variety of voltages ranging from around 7 to 24. The higher the voltage, the more powerful the tool (and the more money it costs). For most remodeling, a 14-volt model is ideal. Spend a little more money to purchase an extra rechargeable battery, so the drill won't run out of power in the middle of a project. A cordless drill/driver is handy for odd jobs and is probably most useful as a power screwdriver, especially when hanging drywall. To equip a drill as a screwdriver,

buy a **magnetic bit holder** and a variety of **screwdriver bits.**

One of the nicest features most cordless drill/drivers have is a clutch, which causes the drill to slip out of gear when it reaches a certain amount of torque. This helps prevent overdriving screws and stripping out the holes or the screwheads.

A **router** and a variety of **router bits** are useful for shaping decorative moldings and cutting mortises for door hinges.

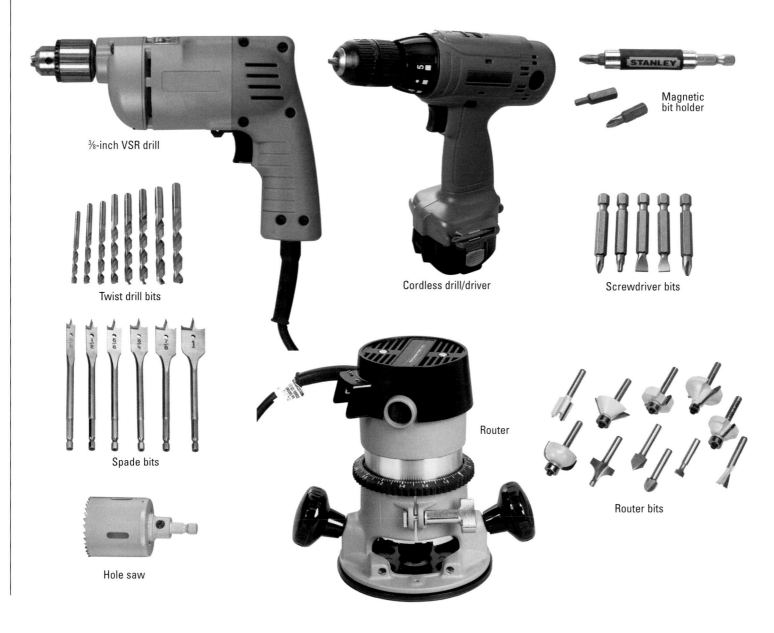

⅜-inch VSR drill

Twist drill bits

Spade bits

Hole saw

Cordless drill/driver

Router

Magnetic bit holder

Screwdriver bits

Router bits

Getting the most out of a drill/driver and router

Clutch adjustment: To keep from over- or underdriving screws, adjust the clutch on a cordless drill/driver. Start with a setting that is a little too light, then gradually increase it until the tool slips when the screw is at the proper depth.

Decorative cuts: Invest in a few edge-forming bits and you can use a router to create almost any molding shape you want. Most edge formers come equipped with a ball-bearing pilot that rides along the edge of the workpiece.

Hinge mortising: Use a ½-inch straight bit to rout mortises for door hinges. You can even purchase hinges with rounded corners that match the radius of the bit, saving you the job of squaring the corners of the mortise.

STANLEY PRO TIP: **Predrill screw holes to prevent splitting**

When you drive a screw without a pilot hole, there are four potential outcomes, three of them bad. If the screw hits a knot or other odd grain in the wood, the head of the screw might twist off; you might overdrive the screw, stripping the hold it has in the wood; or the wood might split. Of course, the screw could go in properly, but don't take chances. Always drill pilot holes.

If appearance is important, you may want to countersink or counterbore the hole. Countersinking makes a shallow depression at the top of the screw hole so the screw head can be driven flush without crushing wood fibers at the surface. Counterboring goes even deeper; you cover the screw head with a wooden plug.

Counterboring and countersinking are done with the same specialized attachment that fits over a regular drill bit. Sized for various screw heads, the attachments allow you to adjust the predrilling depth.

Lay out the center of the hole with an X. Mark the exact center of the X with an awl to keep the drill bit from wandering off target.

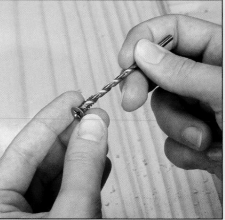

To select the proper size bit for a pilot hole, hold the bit in front of the screw. Match the diameter of the bit to the minor diameter of the screw; that is, the diameter of the screw minus the depth of the threads.

FINISHING TOOLS

Installing and finishing drywall and repairing plaster requires a specialized set of tools. For laying out and guiding the cuts on a sheet of drywall, nothing beats a **drywall square.** After laying out the cut lines, make them with a **utility knife.** For interior cutouts, such as those around electrical boxes, use a **jab saw** to plunge through the drywall and saw out the scrap piece. For slight trimming, such as when you want to plane an edge flush at a corner, use a **Surform® plane.**

Once the drywall is installed, the finishing process begins with spreading joint compound over the fasteners, and taping and spreading compound across the joints between the drywall sheets. The tools used for spreading the compound are called taping or **drywall knives.** These come in a variety of widths. For most purposes a 6-inch, a 10-inch, and a 12-inch will handle the task. Along with the knives, get a **mud pan** to carry a supply of joint compound (often called "mud").

The final stage of finishing drywall consists of smoothing the dried compound. The traditional method involves sanding with **abrasive paper,** which is fine for small jobs. For larger expanses of drywall, invest in **sanding screens** and a **holder** to mount them on. Some holder models have a dust pickup that attaches to the hose of a **shop vacuum.** Be sure to replace the filter in your vacuum with one designed to handle drywall dust. For an almost dust-free environment, smooth the walls with a **drywall sponge,** which has a tough abrasive plastic layer laminated to one side.

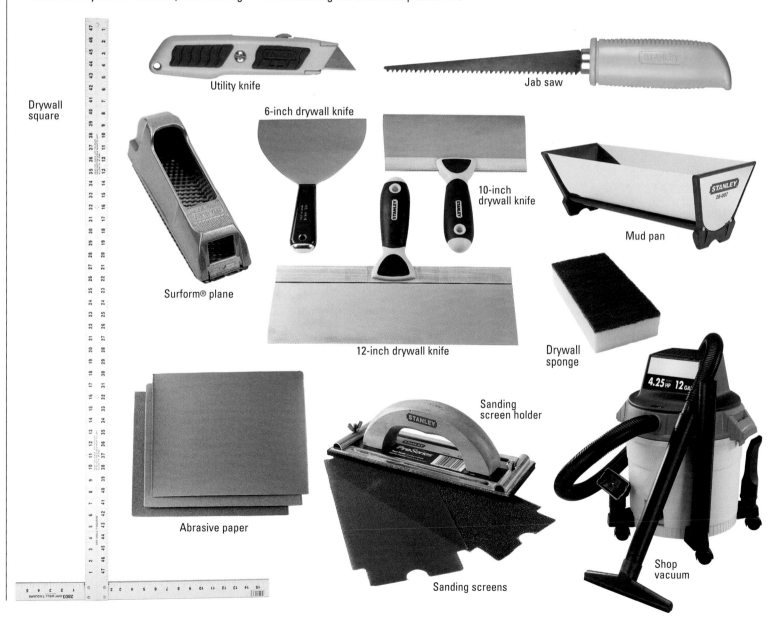

Drywall square

Utility knife

Jab saw

6-inch drywall knife

Surform® plane

10-inch drywall knife

12-inch drywall knife

Mud pan

Drywall sponge

Abrasive paper

Sanding screen holder

Sanding screens

Shop vacuum

ACCESSORIES

Several items make working with hand and power tools easier, starting with one or two **extension cords.** Purchase heavy-duty ones—the wires should be 12 gauge. Lighter weight cords could overheat, posing a fire or shock hazard, and they will rob the tools of the power they need.

Sawhorses hold lumber at a comfortable working height. You can create an impromptu worktable by nailing a sheet of plywood between two horses. Wooden horses are heavier than metal models, but they do have some advantages. You can nail a couple of 2×4s across them for added stability, and should you happen to cut into one, you won't damage your saw blade. Metal sawhorses are sturdy, lighter, and often fold for easy storage. If you use a metal sawhorse, bolt a 2×4 on top of the crosspiece (countersinking the bolt heads) to help prevent damage to saw blades.

If you're doing any work overhead, a **stepladder** provides a safe, comfortable work platform. A 5- or 6-foot ladder will be adequate for most tasks.

A bright **work light** makes a big difference if you are working in dimly lit spaces (where most remodeling projects take place). Halogen models produce a lot of light and often come with adjustable stands. They become very hot when left on for a long time, however, and some models should not be used indoors.

Sawhorses

Extension cord

Work light

6-foot stepladder

3-foot stepladder

PRO TIP: **Save your sawhorses**

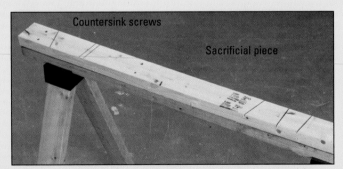

Countersink screws

Sacrificial piece

As they age, the top edges of most sawhorses become scarred from use. To make your horses last longer, add sacrificial pieces of wood to the top edges. These can be screwed in place and replaced as needed. Be sure to countersink the screws deeply to keep saw blades from striking the screw heads.

Storing and protecting your tools

Caring for your power tools is easy— just keep them away from dust and moisture. One handy way to keep them organized is to store them in plastic milk crates. The crates have handles for easy carrying, and they serve as impromptu step stools.

Hand tools with cutting edges— handsaws, chisels, and planes— require a little more care to prevent nicking and dulling the edges. Store them neatly and separately rather than jumbled in a drawer or toolbox. Hooks on a pegboard work well for storing chisels and saws. Get in the habit of storing planes on their sides to protect the blade.

A great way to protect the cutting edges of your chisels and handsaws is to purchase a length of $\frac{1}{2}$-inch-diameter clear plastic tubing. Slit the tubing open with a utility knife and cut it to lengths to fit your tools.

RENTING

Several tools are useful to remodelers but are too expensive to own for the few times they will be used. Check with a local rental shop, hardware store, or home center to see what is available for rent by the hour, day, or week. Among the tools you may find useful for remodeling projects is a **table saw.** This stationary power tool makes ripping lumber to width easy. It is also good for cutting plywood and other sheet stock, and for making precise crosscuts.

A **drywall hoist** takes a lot of the stress and strain out of hanging drywall. If you have enough space to make use of one, renting a hoist is well worth the money spent. For drop ceilings, nothing beats a **laser level** for setting the initial layout line around the perimeter of the room.

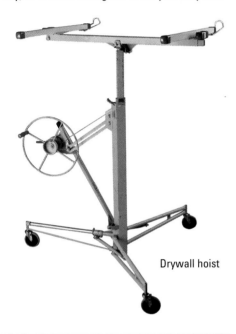

Drywall hoist

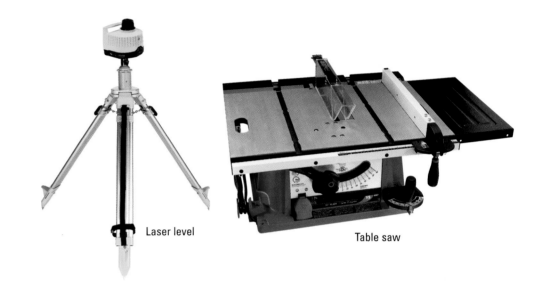

Laser level

Table saw

Build a stable work platform

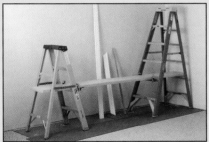

Most overhead work can be accomplished using a ladder, but there are times when a larger elevated work platform is needed. The pros often use a scaffold. You can accomplish the same thing by resting a 2×12 across the rungs of two stepladders. Clamp the board to the ladders to prevent it from slipping. For safety, don't use this method to span more than about 12 feet.

Choosing a tool pouch

A tool pouch may seem like a luxury, something only pros really need. And it's true, you probably don't need a double-bag tool rig with built-in padded suspenders.

Yet even if you are a weekend warrior, a good tool pouch is the best timesaving and frustration-preventing tool you can buy. Without one, your work will be constantly interrupted as you fetch tools you forgot to have on hand.

To be truly quick on the draw, purchase a compartmentalized side pouch with its own belt. The exact configuration of these pouches varies but most have a large pocket with a smaller pocket attached to the outside. The large pocket has plenty of room for your layout square and tape measure plus your chalk line when you need one. The smaller pouch is for nails or screws. Flanking the smaller pocket you should find two pockets: one sized to hold your utility knife, the other for a chisel or putty knife.

Attached to the flanking pockets you'll usually find four narrow pockets suitable for pencils and nail sets.

Most nail pouches have loops that hold a hammer, but few carpenters use it for that. It's much more efficient to have a separate hammer loop on your hammer-hand side with the pouch on the other side. If you will be driving screws, you can replace the hammer loop with a drill/driver holster.

CHOOSING MATERIALS

Many homeowners today can find two or three home centers plus a local lumberyard within easy driving distance. This competition is a boon to do-it-yourselfers and remodelers, offering a quantity and quality of materials that is truly remarkable.

Price, naturally, is the first thing you'll look for when deciding where to shop. But it isn't the only consideration. While the quality of hardware doesn't vary much, the quality of lumber and plywood does. Choose a store that lets you sort through its stacks when selecting pieces. You'll soon discover which stores are consistently well-stocked with quality materials. A good yard or home center allows you to return unused materials.

Think about how you will get your materials home. Even if you have a heavy-duty roof rack, a room's worth of drywall will seriously overload your car's suspension. Many local lumberyards deliver for free if you order a minimum dollar amount, are within a certain distance, and are willing to wait a few days until one of their trucks is driving your way. Otherwise there may be a delivery fee. As another option, some home centers rent small flatbed trucks by the hour, so you can haul your own load.

What to buy

Most remodeling projects focus on walls—either building new ones or modifying existing ones. So the materials you'll use are those of basic carpentry: framing lumber for the wall's structure, drywall or other sheet stock for the skin, and moldings to provide a finished look. To put everything together you'll need a variety of fasteners. To complete a project you'll need joint compound to finish the seams in the drywall, maybe a door or two, and paint.

Where to find help

As you plan your remodeling project, talk to the people at your local lumberyard, whether it's a big home center or a locally owned store. The workers at the lumber desk can be especially helpful; often they are former tradespeople who made their living using the same tools and materials you will be using.

Spending extra time to select top-quality materials prevents frustration in the long run.

CHAPTER PREVIEW

Lumber
page 28

Trim
page 30

Drywall
page 31

With your plans decided, it's time to select the materials that will make them a reality. In this chapter you'll learn how to choose the right materials when you visit the lumberyard or home center.

Sheet stock
page 32

Fasteners, adhesives, and fillers
page 34

LUMBER

Lumber makes up the structure of most houses and no doubt plays a big part in your remodeling project. For framing (building the skeleton of walls), most of the wood you use will be 2× ("two by") material. When it was sawed to size, the wood you are purchasing was in fact about 2 inches thick. But ½ inch of its thickness was lost to shrinkage and planing. So the pieces that reach consumers actually are about 1½ inches thick.

The same holds true with regard to the width of wood pieces—they are narrower than their stated sizes. The stated length, however, is usually close or slightly longer than the actual length. Thus a piece labeled 2×4×8 feet (a typical stud size) is really 1½ inches thick, 3½ inches wide, and 8 feet long.

For the most part, you will be using 2×4s and 2×6s. Occasionally you may need something wider, such as a 2×8, 2×10, or even 2×12. Note that on the wider pieces (2×8, 2×10, 2×12), the width is about ¾ inch narrower than stated; on the smaller pieces, the width is ½ inch less.

Many home centers have two or more grades of lumber. The grades indicate the relative quality of the wood. The better the grade (#1 vs. #2), the fewer defects the pieces have, and the higher the price. Usually you will not need the greater strength that characterizes better grades of lumber, but better grades also are more consistently straight, a desirable quality.

Along with grade, the species of the wood makes a difference in the price. In the Northeast, for instance, lesser grades of 2×4 studs are lumped into a category called SPF, which stands for spruce, pine, and fir. The better studs are douglas fir or occasionally hemlock. These two species command a higher price because they tend to yield stronger, better-quality wood.

Steel studs match the size of wooden studs and are used for similar situations. They are light and fireproof and are cut with tin snips and attached with screws.

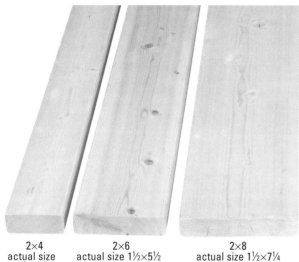

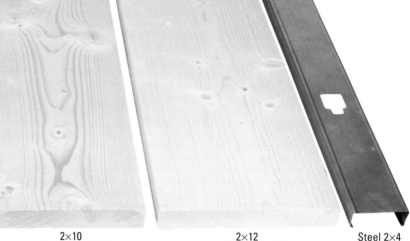

| 2×4 actual size 1½×3½ | 2×6 actual size 1½×5½ | 2×8 actual size 1½×7¼ | 2×10 actual size 1½×9¼ | 2×12 actual size 1½×11¼ | Steel 2×4 actual size 1½×3½ |

Which grade to buy?

For most remodeling projects, buying a higher grade of lumber is a waste of money. If you have the opportunity to select each piece of wood, which is usually the case at home centers or lumberyards, you can avoid the worst pieces of the lesser grades and return home with pieces of wood suited to your purposes. High-grade lumber may be worth the extra cost if the wood will remain visible in the finished result.

The grade stamp on a piece of lumber tells you where the wood came from and what grade it received at the mill. The lower the grade number, the higher the quality of the wood. Instead of a number, 2×4s are often stamped "STUD" to indicate they are suitable for this purpose. "Hem-Fir" means the wood is either hemlock or fir, two equally strong species. The W means the wood was graded under Western Wood Product Association rules, and 134 is the number assigned to the mill where the wood was processed.

Selecting lumber

Look for defects: Start by looking over each piece for obvious defects. Tight knots are no problem for framing lumber. Reject pieces with knot holes or knots that are loose enough to move with your fingers. Also reject pieces with checks (splits and cracks) and wane (missing corners or edges).

Check for straightness: If a piece seems free of defects, hold it at one end and sight along the edges to see if the piece is straight. A slight warp is OK, but reject boards that are severely bowed or twisted.

Remove hazards: As you handle stock, watch for staples and other metal hardware that may be embedded in the wood, waiting to ambush your saw blade. While not a reason to reject a good piece of lumber, staples are a hazard. Remove them immediately after purchase.

Buying the right length

Most framing lumber comes in lengths starting at 8 feet and increasing in 2-foot increments. Keep this in mind as you make your shopping list; you may be able to cut a single long piece into the shorter pieces you need. For example, if you need several 5-foot 2×4s, cut 10-footers into two 5-foot sections, rather than cutting down 8-footers and leaving 3-foot-long scraps.

Many suppliers stock what they call precut studs. These are 2×4s that are 92⅝ inches long (just under 8 feet), the right size for 8-foot walls (the top and bottom plates add 4½ inches to the overall wall height, flooring and ceiling drywall subtract an inch or so).

Marking your purchases

As you select lumber, note the use of each piece, according to your materials list *(page 9)*; for example, a wall stud or a bottom plate. As you place each piece on the cart, use a lumber crayon to write on the wood itself exactly what it is for. This prevents the frustration of spending several hours at the lumberyard selecting stock for your project, getting it home, and then needing to sort it all over again.

TRIM

Along with framing lumber, you will need thinner pieces to use as trim. Trim eases the transitions between surfaces, such as walls and ceilings, and disguises gaps and other irregularities. It also adds a look of style and completeness to an interior remodeling project.

Trim usually takes the form of various moldings (strips of wood cut with decorative profiles). These can be as ornate or as plain as you like. Most home centers have a selection of basic profiles from which to choose. They also have catalogs if you'd like to order other profiles. If you are more ambitious, you can save some money by purchasing nominal 1× boards (actually

¾ inches thick) and cutting your own molding using a router equipped with an edge-forming bit.

Where moldings are used

Molding is typically applied around door and window frames, where it is called **casing.** It also serves as a transition between wall and floor, **baseboard,** and between wall and ceiling, **crown molding.** For an added touch, attach a chair rail to the wall about 3 feet off the floor, or a **picture frame molding** about 26 inches down from the ceiling. Sometimes paneling called wainscoting is applied below the chair rail.

Materials

Most moldings are made from solid wood, typically pine or other softwoods. They are available in either stain or paint grade. Stain-grade moldings are cut from long, knot-free lengths of wood and are meant to be finished with stain, a clear wood finish, or both. Paint-grade moldings are usually cheaper and are made up of short sections of wood joined end to end. Paint-grade moldings made of medium density fiberboard (MDF) are also available. Some larger, more ornate crown moldings are made of polystyrene covered with a gypsum face or of polyurethane foam.

TRIM OPTIONS

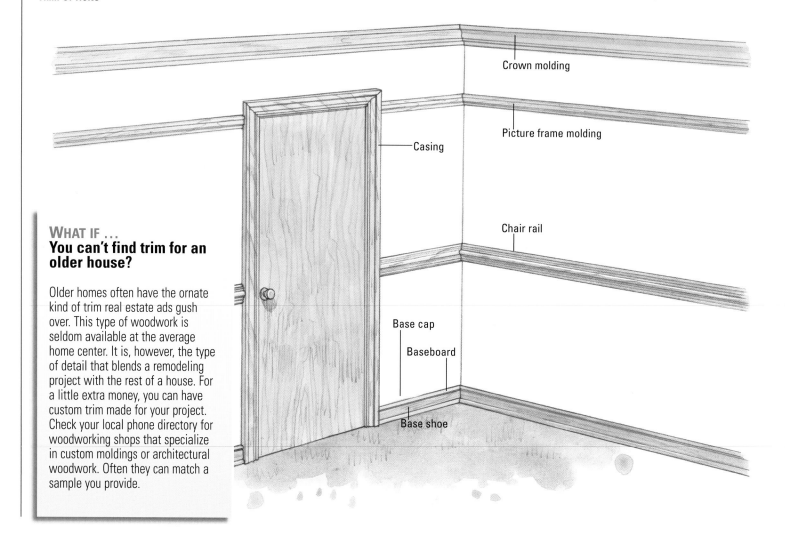

Crown molding

Picture frame molding

Casing

Chair rail

Base cap

Baseboard

Base shoe

WHAT IF ...
You can't find trim for an older house?

Older homes often have the ornate kind of trim real estate ads gush over. This type of woodwork is seldom available at the average home center. It is, however, the type of detail that blends a remodeling project with the rest of a house. For a little extra money, you can have custom trim made for your project. Check your local phone directory for woodworking shops that specialize in custom moldings or architectural woodwork. Often they can match a sample you provide.

DRYWALL

The wall surface found in most modern homes is a material called drywall, made of a thick layer of gypsum sandwiched between two layers of paper. The paper actually gives the material its strength. Drywall commonly comes in sheets that are 4 feet wide and 8 feet to 16 feet long. It comes in four thicknesses—¼ inch, ⅜ inch, ½ inch, and ⅝ inch. The long edges of the sheets are tapered to help create a flat seam where two pieces adjoin. The ends are left at full thickness.

The longer the pieces you can use, the fewer end-to-end seams you'll have to tape and fill. This convenience comes at a price: The added length means added weight and decreased mobility. Recruit a helper or two before you start to hang (attach) the drywall, and make sure it fits into the work area before you order a load of 16-foot pieces.

Most walls and ceilings are covered with ½-inch drywall. In cheaper construction, you'll occasionally find ⅜-inch. The thinner size also works well when covering old plaster walls to renew them. For top quality, ⅝-inch drywall is the way to go. It is stiffer than the thinner sheets, which makes for a flatter wall. It also has more sound-deadening qualities. Your local building code may require ⅝-inch drywall as fire protection in certain situations, such as a wall between an attached garage and the house. On ceilings, ⅝-inch drywall tends to sag less than thinner sheets, especially when attached to 24-inch on center trusses.

To cover curved surfaces, use two layers of ¼-inch drywall (⅜-inch will work if the curve isn't too severe).

Moisture-resistant (MR) drywall (sometimes called greenboard because its paper facings have a greenish tint) is meant for use in damp locations such as in bathrooms or laundry rooms. MR drywall is somewhat more flexible than regular drywall and tends to sag, especially when damp. It should not be used for ceilings unless the joists are spaced 12 inches on center.

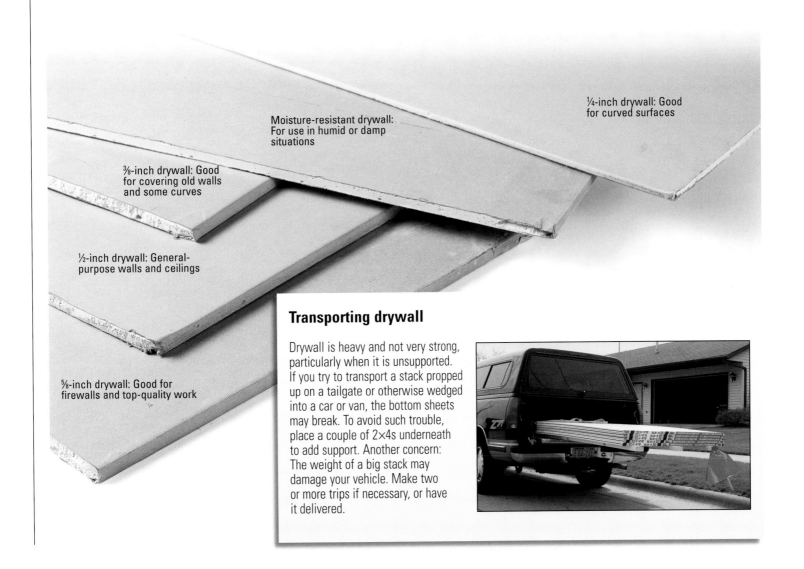

¼-inch drywall: Good for curved surfaces

Moisture-resistant drywall: For use in humid or damp situations

⅜-inch drywall: Good for covering old walls and some curves

½-inch drywall: General-purpose walls and ceilings

⅝-inch drywall: Good for firewalls and top-quality work

Transporting drywall

Drywall is heavy and not very strong, particularly when it is unsupported. If you try to transport a stack propped up on a tailgate or otherwise wedged into a car or van, the bottom sheets may break. To avoid such trouble, place a couple of 2×4s underneath to add support. Another concern: The weight of a big stack may damage your vehicle. Make two or more trips if necessary, or have it delivered.

SHEET STOCK

Along with framing lumber, trim, and drywall, you may find use for different types of sheet stock. This category includes plywood, particleboard, oriented strand board (OSB), medium density fiberboard (MDF), and medium density overlay (MDO). These products come in 4-foot × 8-foot sheets, in thicknesses ranging from ⅛ inch to 1¼ inch (although the thickest and the thinnest sizes may be harder to find). Along with full sheets, many home centers offer quarter and half sheets.

Plywood, an engineered wood product, is made of a sandwich of thin layers of wood called plies or veneers. Each successive ply is laid with the grain running at 90 degrees to the previous layer. The resulting sheet is dimensionally stable and very strong.

Construction plywood, made of softwood veneers, is graded according to the quality of the veneers that make up the two outside faces. These grades, from best to worst, are A, B, C, and D. One of the most common grades of plywood used in construction is **CDX**, meaning the sheet has one face graded C and the other D. The X stands for exterior, referring to the glue with which the veneers are bonded together. This grade is often used for sheathing and roof decking. **AB plywood**, a better grade of plywood,

AB plywood

Oak veneer plywood

CDX plywood

Birch veneer plywood

Reading the plywood stamp

When shopping for construction plywood, look for a grading stamp that says "APA the Engineered Wood Association." The information on this stamp varies according to the intended use of the panel. For example, if the plywood is graded for sheathing outside walls, it will include the stud spacing on which it should be attached. For interior remodeling, the appearance of the face veneers is most important. Here are the characteristics of each face grade:

A—A smooth, paintable veneer free of knots and possessing only neatly made repairs that are parallel to the grain. It could be finished with a clear coat (rather than paint).

B—A solid-surface veneer that allows only small round knots, patches, and round repairs. Acceptable for the inside surfaces of a painted shelving unit.

C—Allows small knots, knotholes, and patches. Probably not used for an exposed face inside the house unless you are going for a rustic look. The lowest grade allowed for permanent exterior exposure.

D—This veneer can include large knots and knotholes. Acceptable only for a hidden face, such as the surface of a sheathing panel that faces inside the wall.

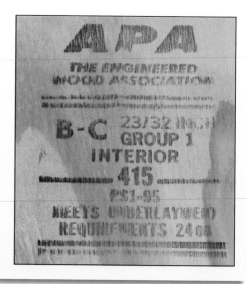

is a good choice for shelving and utility cabinets.

Hardwood plywood is faced with hardwood veneers and is used primarily for furniture and cabinetry. Home centers usually carry **oak and birch veneer plywood**. If you want another species, such as cherry, you can order it through a home center or contact a plywood distributor (look under "plywood" in the phone directory).

Other sheet goods are not as recognizable as wood, though they are wood products. **Particleboard** is made of coarser wood particles. It is commonly used as floor underlayment and occasionally for inexpensive cabinets (often with a vinyl wood-print veneer). It also is frequently used as the bottom layer for countertops. **OSB,** another engineered sheet made of bigger pieces of wood, is stronger than either MDF or particleboard, though not

as strong as plywood, and is commonly used for sheathing and roof decking. MDF is made of fine wood fibers that have been pressed and glued together. The resulting sheets are very smooth and flat. MDF paints well and is a good choice for interior shelving and painted cabinetry. **MDO** has a paper face designed to take paint beautifully. It is commonly used to make outdoor signs.

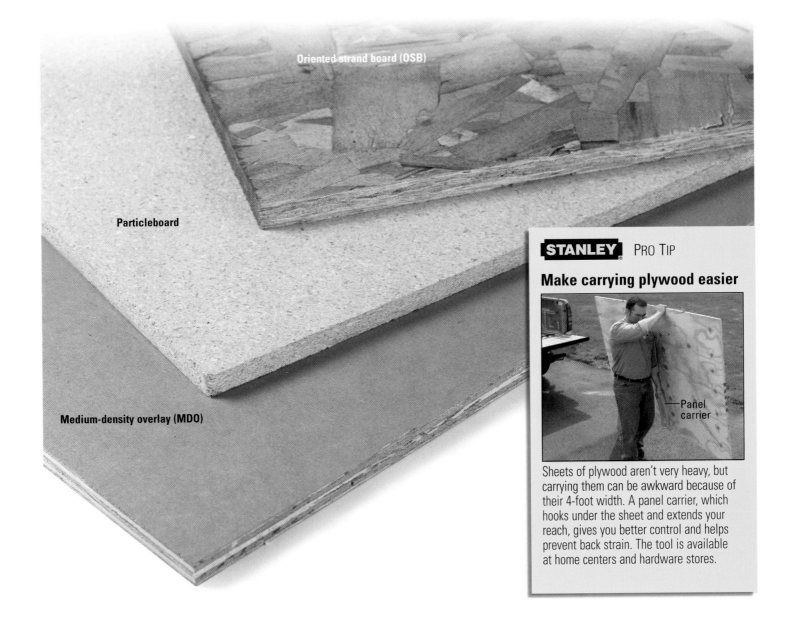

Oriented strand board (OSB)

Particleboard

Medium-density overlay (MDO)

STANLEY PRO TIP

Make carrying plywood easier

Panel carrier

Sheets of plywood aren't very heavy, but carrying them can be awkward because of their 4-foot width. A panel carrier, which hooks under the sheet and extends your reach, gives you better control and helps prevent back strain. The tool is available at home centers and hardware stores.

FASTENERS, ADHESIVES, AND FILLERS

Home centers offer hundreds of different types of fasteners. Most interior remodeling projects, however, require only about half a dozen different types and sizes of nails and screws.

Even the lowly nail presents many choices: There are over 30 styles available; most have a specific purposes such as attaching flooring or roofing. For interior remodeling, you will probably need only three or four types. For framing, you'll need **16d common** nails to attach the studs (the vertical pieces of lumber) to the plates (the horizontal pieces). You'll also use these 3½-inch-long nails to anchor the plates to the floor. You'll need **8d common** nails, which are 2½ inches long, mostly for toenailing (nailing at an angle through the one piece of wood into the face of another piece). You'll need **10d common** nails (3 inches long) for general nailing, such as fastening two studs face-to-face.

For attaching trim and hanging doors, you'll need **finishing nails.** These nails have a small head that allows them to be driven below the surface of the wood and can be hidden with dabs of wood putty. A supply of 4d, 6d, 8d, and 16d finishing nails should handle any trim you are likely to install.

You'll also find it handy to have screws of different lengths on hand. These days, the most common screws used are general-purpose or **drywall screws.** These black screws have a phillips head (the drive slot is X-shaped) and are available with coarse or fine threads. The coarse-thread variety

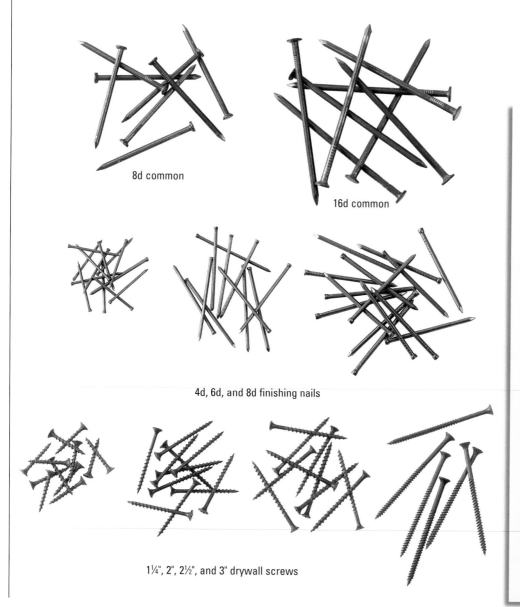

8d common

16d common

4d, 6d, and 8d finishing nails

1¼", 2", 2½", and 3" drywall screws

NAIL SIZES

Nails are sized by the "penny" abbreviated "d," as in 8d nails, which refers to length. The origin of the term is fuzzy, but one common explanation is that when nails were first mass-produced, they were sold by the hundred. The designation told how many pennies each nail cost per hundred.

Penny size	Length in inches
2d	1
3d	1¼
4d	1½
5d	1⅝
6d	2
7d	2⅛
8d	2½
10d	3
12d	3¼
16d	3½
28d	4
30d	4½
40d	5
50d	5½
60d	6

drives in faster, while the fine-thread screw has slightly more holding power. In practice, you probably won't notice much difference between the two. Drywall screws are meant to be power-driven with an electric drill or a cordless drill/driver. For hanging drywall, you'll need 1¼-inch screws. Have some 1⅝-inch, 2-inch, 2½-inch, and 3-inch screws on hand for general use.

Adhesives and fillers

Along with mechanical fasteners, a wide variety of chemical adhesives and fillers helps you join things together. Some, such as vinyl flooring adhesive, are formulated to do specific jobs. Others, such as **construction adhesive,** can be used with a wide variety of materials together. It's commonly used to adhere drywall to the wall framing. Traditional adhesives such as **yellow wood glue** are used to install moldings and other trim.

As you finish up your remodeling job, you'll need some filler materials. **Joint compound** fills the seams and covers screw or nail holes in drywall. It is commonly sold in 5-gallon buckets, though smaller quantities are available. **Caulk** is often used for disguising gaps in moldings. For hiding the nailheads in trim that will be painted, use cellulose fiber **wood filler.** If you will be staining the trim, use wood filler available in colors to match, or a **wax crayon wood filler.** Keep in mind that the match is always approximate; don't expect filled holes in stained trim to disappear.

Construction adhesive

Yellow wood glue

Caulk

Wood filler

Wax crayon wood filler

Joint compound

STANLEY PRO TIP

Carrying and storing fasteners

The boxes that most fasteners come in are great for getting them home from the store. Once open, however, it is only a matter of time before their seams burst, leaving you with a mess. One of the best ways to store and carry fasteners is in a parachute bag. These durable totes have multiple compartments for holding a variety of fasteners and a drawstring you can cinch to prevent spills.

DEMOLITION

The first stage of a remodeling job typically is demolition—tearing out the old to make way for the new. Demolition is messy work. Unless you're remodeling the entire house, you'll want to make every effort to contain the dust and debris in your work area. The first part of this chapter explains how to seal off the work area.

Despite the mess, demolition can be rewarding. It moves along quickly, progress is quite visible, and knocking things apart can be rather fun—remember how flattening a sand castle was more fun than building it?

Demolition with forethought
Before you start swinging a sledgehammer, however, consider whether you want to salvage anything from the existing room. Some things may be worth reusing. Wood moldings, for example, can be difficult to match, and even if the profiles are readily available, you can save money by reusing them when possible. Later in this chapter you will learn techniques and tips for removing moldings from walls and nails from moldings without damaging either the walls or the molding.

Save the lumber
Framing lumber also has potential for reuse, but watch out for hidden nails. Doors, too, can be worth salvaging, even if you don't need them for your new design. For example, a flat hollow-core door laid across a pair of sawhorses makes a great temporary table.

Some communities have architectural salvage yards that buy and sell used house parts, so you may profit a little from your labors by selling used pieces. Some communities have a building material bank, where low-income families procure materials for renovating their homes at little or no cost. Check your local phone listings.

Removing drywall and plaster
Removing the wall surface, whether drywall or plaster, doesn't take any special skills. The goal simply is to remove the material and dispose of it while creating as little mess as possible.

Demolition is messy but rewarding work. It moves quickly, progress is quite visible, and it's fun.

CHAPTER PREVIEW

Preparing the work area
page 38

Removing and saving moldings
page 40

Removing drywall
page 42

Removing plaster
page 44

Demolition creates lots of dust. Be sure to wear a good-quality dust mask and safety glasses or goggles.

Plastic over the doorway helps keep dust out of the rest of the house.

A layer of ¼-inch plywood protects the floors during demolition and construction.

Demolition is a dirty business. However, a small amount of effort invested in containing the mess pays big dividends when it comes time to clean up. Protect the unaltered parts of the house so you don't create extra work.

Removing framing members
page 45

Waste disposal and cleanup
page 47

PREPARING THE WORK AREA

For major remodeling projects, such as removing and building walls, and many simpler tasks, it is worth spending a little time and money to prepare the work area before any work is done. The goal is to isolate the work site as much as possible from the rest of the house. The chief enemy is dust. If you do not seal off the area, you can be sure that remodeling dust will get into everything from your breakfast cereal to your sock drawer.

It is also important to protect the floor in your work area. Don't make the mistake of thinking you can clean the floor later and don't need to protect it until it is time to paint. Construction dust is very hard to expel from the spaces between floorboards and about impossible to clean from carpet. Dropped tools and spills also can easily damage the floor during demolition or construction if you don't protect it.

PRESTART CHECKLIST

☐ **TIME**
About an hour to hang a modest-size (8×10 feet) curtain

☐ **TOOLS**
Saw, staple gun, electric drill/driver, spring clamps

☐ **SKILLS**
Cutting plywood and 1×2 lumber, stapling plastic sheet, power-driving screws

☐ **PREP**
Acquire materials, clear room of furnishings and other household items

☐ **MATERIALS**
20-mil plastic sheet, ¼-inch staples, 2-inch screws, duct tape

1 If you are working over carpet or finished flooring, protect it with a layer of ¼-inch lauan plywood. Cut the pieces to fit and seal their edges with duct tape.

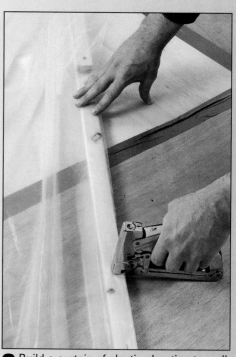

2 Build a curtain of plastic sheeting to wall off your work area. Staple the plastic to a length of 1×2, then roll the plastic around the 1×2 to reinforce the connection.

STANLEY PRO TIP: **Deal with dust**

Blow it away: If the demolition room has a window, open it and prop a box fan in place so it blows out. This will evacuate a lot of the airborne dust.

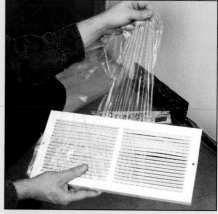

Wrap the registers: Prevent the spread of dust by removing any heating, cooling, or ventilation registers in the demolition room. Wrap them in plastic wrap and replace them.

3 To hang the sheeting, screw the 1×2 to the ceiling. Use a single 1¾-inch screw every 3 feet or so and make sure the screws go into framing. Patching these few holes later is a small price to pay for containing the mess.

4 Tape the edges of the plastic to the floor and to the walls to form a final seal. If needed, create a doorway in the curtain.

5 As a final defense against tracking dust through the house, place a doormat just outside the curtain wall. Shake out the mat frequently when you are working.

Leaving dust behind

The best defense against tracking construction dust around the house is a pair of slippers left outside the entrance to the work area. Leave your dusty work shoes in the work area and slip on the slippers when you leave. This remains a good idea later when it's time to apply joint compound, sand, and paint the walls and ceilings.

CREATE A DOORWAY

You won't need a full wall of sheeting if you are working in a room that is separated from the rest of the house by a door. There you can simply attach plastic sheeting over the doorway as a seal. However, you will still need to create a doorway in the plastic to gain access to the work area. Just cut the sheet by the door opening.

1 When you put up the plastic, leave a fold of about 12–18 inches where the doorway will be. After the plastic is up, slit the sheet vertically to make two flaps.

2 To seal the flaps, fold them together and clip them with two or three spring clamps.

REMOVING AND SAVING MOLDINGS

The first pieces to come off a wall are the last pieces to be installed—the moldings and other pieces of trim. It can be worth your while to remove them carefully so they can be reused, especially when dealing with the ornate woodwork found in older homes. Matching new replacements to old woodwork can be expensive.

The challenge is to remove the moldings without damaging them or anything else that will remain. Work slowly and methodically, prying the pieces loose from the nails that anchor them in place.

Nails present two problems. First, if the molding has been painted, you probably won't be able to see where the nails are located. Second, even if you know where the nails are, you won't be able to get at them because their heads will have been set beneath the surface of the molding. There are two ways to deal with these problems: You can pry the molding away from the wall, then pull out the nails from the back or cut them off; or you can <u>drive the nails through</u> the molding. Don't try to back the nails out. Their heads likely will chip the face of the molding as they are driven out.

PRESTART CHECKLIST

☐ **TIME**
About 10 to 15 minutes per piece of molding, depending on length

☐ **TOOLS**
Putty knife, 3-inch drywall knife, flat bar, hammer, nail set, end nips, file

☐ **SKILLS**
Prying, driving nails, cutting nails, filing

1 Beginning at one end of a piece of molding, gently work a putty knife between the molding and the wall. You may have to tap the putty knife gently with a hammer to force it between the wall and molding.

2 As the molding loosens, work in a 3-inch drywall knife from underneath or from the other edge. Continue to pry gently along the length of the molding until you are able to see the nails that fasten the molding in place.

DRIVE THE NAILS THROUGH

One approach to removing trim is to drive the nails through the molding. This frees the molding and eliminates the problem of what to do with the nails protruding from a piece you want to save. This method also eliminates the possibility of damaging or breaking the molding while you pry on it. The drawback is that you can easily split moldings—especially narrow ones—by driving the nails through. And in some cases, if the trim is a hardwood, such as oak, it can be difficult to drive the nails further.

First locate the nails. On woodwork that has been stained or coated with a clear finish, look for telltale spots of filler. On painted moldings, you may have to first pry them away from the wall as described above. Once you find the nails, drive them through the molding with a hammer and a nail set. Use a small-diameter nail set to avoid enlarging the hole.

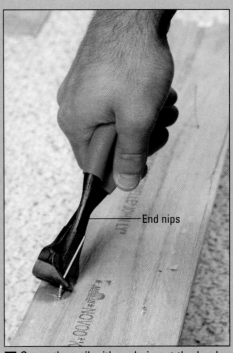

Scrap plywood

End nips

3 As the gaps widen, slip a flat bar behind the molding. Work along the length, gently prying the piece away from its home. Back up the bar with a scrap of ¼-inch plywood to avoid damaging the wall or floor.

4 Free one end of the molding, then work along the rest of the piece, prying where each nail is located.

5 Grasp the nail with end nips at the back of the molding and pull it sideways, being careful not to dent the edges of the molding.

Dealing with stubborn nails

The small heads of most finishing nails pull easily through the back of molding, but sometimes, especially with older nails in hardwood molding, you can't pull nails without causing damage. In that case, clip off the nails with end nips and file away any protruding part of the nail until it is flush with the back of the molding.

WHAT IF…
The paint acts like glue?

Paint can act like glue, sticking moldings together, especially in a room that has numerous coats of paint. The parts that are stuck can easily break off, particularly if they are older wood, which can be quite brittle. Paint often disguises the seams between moldings, making it difficult to see which parts of a molding are separate pieces of wood. If you have this problem, gently loosen and remove the excess paint with a paint scraper before you attempt to remove the moldings. Use your utility knife to cut through paint seams between moldings. Work slowly and carefully to avoid slips that can mar the molding.

REMOVING DRYWALL

After the moldings are out of the way, the next step is to remove the drywall or plaster from the wall (see *page 44*). Before you start smashing the wall with a hammer, you need to know if there are any pipes, ducts, or wiring inside *(see page 11)*.

This is a messy job, so work carefully to avoid creating undue debris and dust. Remove drywall in large pieces. Start near the top of the wall and work down, prying the drywall free of its fasteners as you go. Drywall is inexpensive, so don't try to save it for reuse. The wall studs are worth saving unless the drywall was attached with construction adhesive. Sometimes you can scrape the adhesive off with a putty knife, but you'll probably decide it isn't worth the work.

Be sure to wear a dust mask rated for fine dust, not just a "nuisance dust" mask. A fine-dust mask has two straps and is thicker than a nuisance mask.

For more on cleanup and waste disposal, see *page 47*.

1 Almost every wall in a house is likely to have electrical wires in it, so even if you don't find evidence of wiring, **turn off the circuit at the service panel.** When you are sure all switches and receptacles in the wall are dead, remove their cover plates.

2 To make finishing easier, make a clean break between the wall you are removing and other walls. Run a utility knife firmly down both corners of the wall. It may take two or three passes to cut completely through the joint compound and tape. Do this on both sides of the wall to be removed.

PRESTART CHECKLIST

☐ **TIME**
About 1 to 2 hours per sheet (32 square feet) of drywall from start to final cleanup

☐ **TOOLS**
Hammer, flat bar, end nips, utility knife, screw drill/driver (for removing drywall screws), reciprocating saw (for removing parts of walls), handsaw

☐ **SKILLS**
Prying, pulling nails, removing screws, cutting with a reciprocating saw

☐ **PREP**
Isolate the work site to contain the mess; determine what utilities may be contained within the wall

SAFETY FIRST
Turn off the circuit at the service panel

Before doing any electrical work, you must turn off the electrical circuit at the main service panel. Inside the panel, the circuits should be labeled. If they are, flip the appropriate circuit breaker to the off position or remove the fuse. To make sure the power is off, plug a table lamp into both outlets in every receptacle in the wall you will work on. If there is a switch or switches in the room, flip them for every outlet — sometimes one outlet in a receptacle is controlled by a switch and the other isn't.

If the panel has no labels, plug a radio into an outlet in the wall to be removed. Turn it up loud. Flip circuit breakers or remove fuses until the radio goes off. Then test each outlet.

WHAT IF ...
There is insulation in the wall?

Even if the wall you are removing is not an outside wall, you may find insulation inside. This is because insulation is used to block sound as well as air. Sometimes you will find insulation around plumbing drain pipes to block the sound of rushing water. To remove insulation, wear a long-sleeved shirt, long pants, and a dust mask. Roll it up and seal it in large plastic garbage bags for disposal.

3 Use a hammer to punch a series of holes in the wall near the ceiling. The holes should be a couple of inches high and stretch across the stud bays.

4 Grasp the drywall and pull it free from the studs. If necessary, slip a flat bar inside the wall and pry the drywall away from the studs. Break the sheet into as large pieces as possible. Pick up and haul off scraps of drywall as you work, to keep the site clear.

5 Once the drywall is down, clean up the debris still attached to the studs. Then pull drywall nails or unscrew drywall screws. Even if you plan to dispose of the framing, pulling the fasteners makes the studs safer to handle.

WHAT IF ...
You are removing only part of wall?

Some projects call for removing only part of a wall instead of the entire wall from corner to corner. For example, if you're creating a passageway, you'll leave some wall on each side of the opening.

Sometimes you can plan the project so there is a stud at the point where you want the wall to end. You might even want to adjust your wall length an inch or two to accommodate the nearest stud. Then you can simply cut away the drywall as shown (near right).

If your wall won't end at a stud, cut back the drywall farther to the next stud. Later, while framing the new corner, you will nail a new stud against the old to provide a place to nail or screw the new drywall as shown at far right. **Check for wires and pipes inside the wall before sawing.**

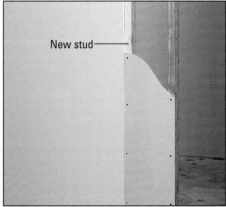

New stud

1 If you have to remove only a portion of the drywall, establish a break line by scribing the drywall along a stud with a utility knife, then cut flush along the stud with a handsaw or reciprocating saw.

2 To provide a place to attach new drywall, screw a new stud alongside the stud you used as a guide for cutting in the previous step. This is much easier than trying to cut back the old drywall halfway onto the existing stud.

REMOVING PLASTER

The walls of many older houses are covered with plaster rather than drywall. Plaster is applied as a wet paste over a series of thin wood strips called lath, which are attached to the wall studs. The plaster is squeezed between these thin pieces, oozing into the wall cavities. When the plaster dries, this ooze, called keys, holds the plaster to the wall.

More recently installed plaster uses an expanded metal mesh rather than wood lath. If you need to cut through the metal lath, tin snips do the job easily. The most difficult part of removing plaster is to do it without damaging adjacent areas.

Before you begin removing plaster, **turn off any nearby circuits at the electrical service panel** *(page 42)*. Remove all receptacle and switch cover plates.

PRESTART CHECKLIST

☐ **TIME**
About 1 to 2 hours per 8-foot section of wall

☐ **TOOLS**
Hammer, pry bar, screw drill/driver (for attaching reinforcing 1×2s), handsaw, reciprocating saw (for removing parts of walls)

☐ **SKILLS**
Prying, pulling nails, cutting with a reciprocating saw and handsaw

☐ **PREP**
Isolate the work site to contain the mess; determine what utilities may be contained within the wall

☐ **MATERIALS**
1×2s to reinforce surrounding plaster, if necessary

1 Plaster is a tough wall surface, but too much pounding and vibration jar it loose. To avoid problems, attach 1×2s at the points that intersect the wall you are removing and at the adjacent ceiling and other walls.

2 If you remove only part of a wall, end at a stud. You can't cut through lath in the middle of a bay without destroying the plaster. To find the end stud, drill ⅛-inch-diameter holes every inch through the waste section of plaster until the drill hits a stud. Attach a reinforcing 1×2 along the stud.

3 Knock the plaster off the wall with a hammer. It is easier to shovel up the loose debris before the lath is mixed in. If some of the lath strips continue past the end stud, use a handsaw or reciprocating saw. Cut them flush to the side of the end stud.

4 As you remove the lath with a flat pry bar, some of the lath nails will stay in the studs; some will come away with the lath. Either way, it's best to remove the nails as you go and pile the lath neatly for disposal.

REMOVING FRAMING MEMBERS

With the drywall or plaster and lath removed, the framing is the last thing to go. It's not difficult to beat the studs from their positions with a sledgehammer, but a neater and safer method is to cut the nails at the bottom, then pry and twist the pieces free. This way, you'll be able to reuse the pieces if you need them; just remember they still have nails in one end. After removing the studs, you can remove the top and bottom plates.

Keep in mind **the directions here apply to nonbearing walls only.** Removing load-bearing walls requires the skills of a master carpenter and sometimes a structural engineer. See *page 10* to learn how to determine if a wall is bearing.

PRESTART CHECKLIST

☐ **TIME**
About 5 to 15 minutes per framing member

☐ **TOOLS**
Reciprocating saw with metal cutting blade, hammer, pry bar

☐ **SKILLS**
Sawing with a reciprocating saw, pulling nails

☐ **PREP**
Remove trim and drywall or plaster and lath

If you don't own a reciprocating saw, consider renting one the day you remove framing.

1 Cut through the nails between the bottom of the stud and the plate with a reciprocating saw. Be sure to use a metal-cutting blade.

2 Knock the bottom of the stud sideways with a hammer to free the bottom. With the bottom loose, twist and lever the stud free of the nails that hold it to the top plate.

WHAT IF ...
You have to remove a doorway?

Use a reciprocating saw to cut the nails at the bottom of one of the two sets of doubled studs the same way you did for single studs. Then lever that leg of the doorway free of the bottom plate. Knock the doubled studs sideways with your hammer to free them from the header and the top plate. Pry the header free of the cripple studs above and the doubled studs on the other side. Then cut the nails holding these doubled studs to the bottom plate and twist this leg free as well.

Removing framing members *(continued)*

Top plate

Top plate

Scrap plywood

Plate to be removed

3 If the bottom and top plates are part of a longer wall, use a handsaw to cut them free from the part of the wall you want to keep. Be careful to avoid marring the ceiling and finished floor if one is in place as you finish the cuts.

4 The top plate consists of two layers of 2×4s. Drive a flat bar between the two layers and pry off the bottom layer. If you are removing a partition wall, the upper top plate overlaps the lower top plate of the main wall. Use a handsaw to cut off the top plate at the main wall.

5 If joists run across the wall you are removing, they probably were nailed down into the top plate. Drive a flat bar between each joist and the top plate and pry the top plate free.

WHAT IF ...
You find utilities in the wall?

Once you open a wall, you'll see exactly what utilities you have to deal with. Then you'll need to decide what to reroute and what to remove. In most cases, there will be some electrical wiring present in a wall. Less frequently, there will be plumbing or possibly some ductwork for your heating and cooling system. If you plan to do your own electrical or plumbing work, see *Stanley Advanced Wiring* and *Stanley Advanced Plumbing* for more information.

If you'd rather not tackle these jobs yourself, hire a professional to remove or reroute the utilities. You may have to wait until the pro can fit you into his schedule. There is, however, an easy way to get wiring out of the way so you can continue working until the electrician arrives. The following approach requires little wiring knowledge.

Reassembled boxes

Start by turning off the electricity by removing the fuse or throwing the circuit breaker that protects them *(page 42)*. Check to make sure the power is off by plugging a light into both outlets in all of the receptacles, and operating all of the switches. Nothing should happen if the power is off.

Next unscrew the receptacles and switches and pull them out of their boxes. Make a sketch of how the wires are connected, especially noting which color wire attaches to which terminal on the device.

Detach the receptacles and switches from the wires. Pull the wires out of the boxes and pull them through any holes in the framing. Remove the boxes from the studs. Run the wires back into the now-loose boxes and reattach them as they were to the various switches and receptacles. Screw the devices back into their boxes and replace the cover plates. If possible, leave the power off to the circuit until the electrician arrives and checks everything out. With the wiring out of the way, you can proceed with demolition.

WASTE DISPOSAL AND CLEANUP

In every remodeling job, several times occur when a major cleanup helps keep a worksite safer and more efficient. One of them is at the end of demolition. When you are finished tearing the place apart, thoroughly clean the site—sweep and vacuum the dust, carry away all the debris, put away tools, and reorganize the site.

This is also the time to make sure the dust barriers are still in place and that you have protected every part of the site that won't be demolished. Cleaning up is a good activity for the end of the day, when you are too tired for any meticulous work but still feel like getting something accomplished.

Double bagging: For small jobs, you can bag the mess and put it out with the trash. But be warned: Construction debris is heavy. Don't overfill containers. Use heavyweight bags; you may even want to double bag to reduce the risk of a spill.

Rent a waste container: For larger jobs, rent a waste container. Check with local authorities to see if you need a permit. If necessary, build or rent a chute to direct debris from a window into the container. Be sure to protect the window through which the debris passes.

Pulling nails as you go

As you remove each piece of wood from a structure, take the time to remove protruding nails. Boards and moldings with nails sticking out are extremely hazardous. Stepping on one can cause a serious injury, and they can snag and rip clothing too.

If you intend to reuse the lumber, mark the location of any nails you have left imbedded in the wood so you won't later cut through them with a saw.

Keep a cat's paw handy for pulling nails as you remove studs and other pieces of wood. A cat's paw is especially handy if the nailheads are deeply imbedded because you can use your hammer to drive the short claw into the wood to get under the head. A pair of end nips also does a good job removing nails.

Use the right filter for the job

A shop vacuum makes quick work of construction dust, but make sure the vacuum filter is up to the job, or you'll simply redistribute the dust. Most stock filters cannot deal with the extremely fine dust generated by remodeling projects. Some vacuum makers sell bags that fit over the regular filters for dealing with fine dust, such as that from joint compound. Or you can retrofit your vacuum with an aftermarket filter.

FRAMING

To many people the word *carpentry* brings to mind framing a wall: nailing 2×4s together one after another to make the skeleton of a house. There is a lot more to carpentry, of course, but the basic skills used in framing make up a substantial part of many interior remodeling projects.

Framing is satisfying work. The pieces go together fairly quickly and progress seems significant. It is important, however, not to get carried away with the speed at which you assemble a wall. After all, every step that follows depends on the quality of the framing. While it is possible to compensate for a wall frame that is twisted or out of square, it is a lot easier to achieve quality work if the frame is flat and true from the start.

Build flat, then set in place

The basic method of framing a wall is to build it flat on the floor, then lift it into place. This allows you to nail the studs in place through the top and bottom plates rather than having to toe-nail them. (Toe-nailing involves driving nails at an angle through the sides and out through the ends of the studs.)

If you were to try to tip a full-height wall into position, however, it would hang up on the ceiling. So you must build the wall 1½ inches short and attach a second top plate to the ceiling. After standing the wall up, you can slide it into place under this second plate and attach it with relative ease.

Another point to keep in mind is that even if you are building a wall with a doorway in it, the bottom plate will run the entire length of the wall to help keep the wall straight until it is nailed in position. Once the wall is attached, the part of the bottom plate that crosses the doorway can be cut away.

Built-ins and basements

Building cabinets into the walls is a surprisingly easy way to add storage space and design flair *(page 62)*.

If it's more living space you need, finishing a basement is one of the most economical ways to get it. No wonder it is such a popular remodeling project. If you are planning a basement remodel, be sure to read Framing with Metal on *page 58* and Insulating a Wall on *page 64*.

If the framing is straight and square, the rest of the job will move ahead with ease.

CHAPTER PREVIEW

Preparing the work site
page 50

Framing a wall
page 52

Framing a doorway
page 56

Framing with metal
page 58

With the top plate in place, you can build the wall on the ground and raise it into place.

Adding blocking in advance to a wall frame makes it easy to attach elements such as chair molding or wall cabinets.

Framing is one of the more exciting parts of remodeling. The pieces go together quickly and progress is quite noticeable.

Enlarging a load-bearing wall opening
page 60

Building cabinets into a wall
page 62

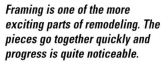

Insulating a wall
page 64

PREPARING THE WORK SITE

The job of putting up a new wall ranges from simple to complex, depending on where the wall is going. The determining factor is whether the wall runs parallel to the ceiling joists or whether it cuts across them. Walls are usually attached to the joists above, so those that cut across the joists are easier to build. This is because their top plates can be nailed through the ceiling to the joists.

The construction of walls that run parallel to the joists is somewhat more involved. Unless you are lucky and your wall falls directly under a joist, you'll have to open up the ceiling to install blocking to attach the top plate. In fact, if moving the wall an inch or two places it under a joist, you should consider doing so.

If you are attaching a top plate through a plaster ceiling into joists, predrill the plate and attach it with 3-inch wood screws.

PRESTART CHECKLIST

☐ **TIME**
About an hour for a simple wall that's perpendicular to the joists

☐ **TOOLS**
Tape measure, chalk line, hammer, circular saw, layout square

☐ **SKILLS**
Measuring, snapping a chalk line, hammering, crosscutting

☐ **PREP**
Complete remodeling plans

☐ **MATERIALS**
2×4 for top plate, 16d nails

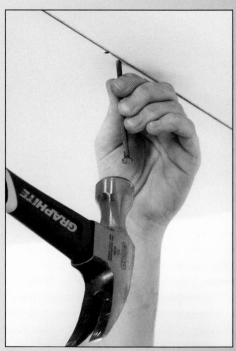

1 Start by locating the ends of the new wall on the ceiling according to the dimensions you worked out on your plan. With a helper, snap a chalk line between the two points.

2 Locate the joists by tapping the ceiling with your knuckles. Joists sound and feel solid; the space between them echoes and sounds hollow. Drive an 8d nail through the ceiling to double-check. If it punches through easily, you've missed the joist; move over an inch and try again.

WHAT IF ...
You don't have a helper?

To snap a chalk line when working alone, drive a nail at one end of your layout. Hook the end of the line on the nail and stretch it tightly at the other end of the layout. Snap the chalk line as usual.

To attach a plate, hold it centered on the layout line. Drive a 3-inch screw through the plate into the joists. (It is easier to hold the plate steady when screwing than when hammering.) Nail the rest of the connections.

3 Once you know where all the joists are, cut a 2×4 to the proper length for the top plate. Measure and transfer the joist locations onto the plate with a tape measure and layout square.

Joist location

4 Drive a 16d nail into the plate where each joist will intersect. It is easier to start the nails now, while the plate is still flat on the floor.

5 With a helper, hold the top plate in place along the chalk line and nail it in place right through the ceiling. If the plate isn't quite straight, nail part of it, then push the offending end into line.

Running a wall parallel to the joists

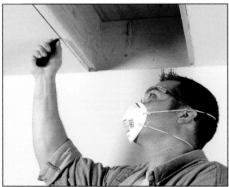

1 Use a handsaw or reciprocating saw to cut away the ceiling flush to the inside faces of the joists where the wall will attach. (For cutting a plaster ceiling, see *page 44.*) Snap a chalk line along the center of each joist, then use a utility knife to cut away a ¾-inch-wide strip of drywall. This will expose surfaces on the joists for attaching the new drywall.

2 Cut blocking to fit snugly between the joists. Use four toenails to attach each block with its wide face down. Use a ⅛-inch diameter bit to predrill the ends of the blocks for the toenails.

3 Nail the blocking in place between the joists. Space the pieces 16 inches on center to provide support for the new drywall, as well as convenient nailing for crown molding.

FRAMING A WALL

Oone way to frame a wall is to install the top and bottom plates and then toe-nail the studs to the plates. But if you have enough space, it's easier to put the pieces together on the floor. This method allows you to nail through the bottom and top plates directly into the bottom and top of the studs, which is much easier than toenailing, especially toenailing over your head. Then you can tip the wall up and move it into position.

To build on the floor, begin by measuring and cutting all the studs to length. Then put the bottom and top plates against each other to mark them for the positions of the studs. Lastly put the studs between the plates and nail the assembly together.

PRESTART CHECKLIST

☐ **TIME**
About 1 hour for an 8×8-foot wall

☐ **TOOLS**
Tape measure, layout square, circular saw, hammer

☐ **SKILLS**
Measuring and marking, crosscutting, driving nails

☐ **PREP**
Install top plate first

☐ **MATERIALS**
2×4s (four for the first 4 feet of wall, three for every 4 feet thereafter, plus top and bottom plates), 16d nails

Whenever you need to attach 2× framing through a plaster wall or ceiling, use 3-inch-long drywall screws instead of nails to avoid breaking the plaster.

A. Build the wall

1 Measure from the underside of the plate on the ceiling to the floor to determine the wall height. Check in several places and use the smallest dimension as the height.

2 Cut the plates and the studs to length. The length of the studs should be 3 inches less than the wall height you just determined. This allows for the thickness of two 2×4 plates (1½ inches each).

WHAT IF...
There isn't enough room to build flat?

If you are working in tight quarters, you'll have to build the wall in place. Start by laying out the plates as described above. Attach the wall top plate to the plate already attached to the ceiling *(pages 50–51)*. Use a plumb bob to locate the bottom plate *(pages 54–55)*. Anchor it to the floor. Cut the studs to fit in between the plates. Toe-nail them in place top and bottom. You may predrill to make driving the nails easier.

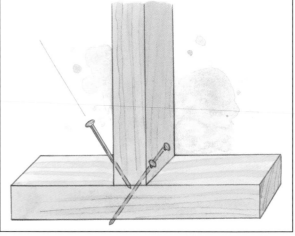

Toenails are driven into the face of a stud at an angle so they come out the end of the stud. Usually three nails are adequate, one driven from one side and two from the other.

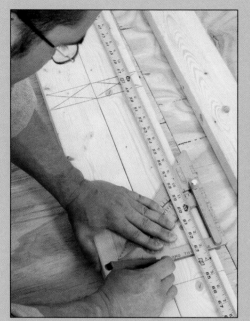

3 Hold the plates side by side to mark the spacing for the studs. The first stud will be offset by ¾ inch; then make a mark every 16 inches to indicate the centers of the studs. Measure ¾ inch on either side of each mark and draw lines to show where the sides of the studs will be.

4 Place the studs on edge in between the plates. If any studs are not perfectly flat, turn them so that any slight gap is at the bottom. Hold them in position one by one and nail them in place through the plates. Make sure the edges of the studs are flush with the edges of the plates.

5 Blocking may be added to the wall to provide a solid nailing surface for moldings or cabinets. If needed, nail blocking between the studs. Position the blocking with the wide face out. Toe-nail one side of each block. Here the pieces are positioned to support a chair rail molding.

SPACING FOR THE STUDS

Laying out the positions of the studs in a wall is a crucial step in construction. Get it right and installing drywall is easy; make a mistake and you'll have problems.

The most common spacing is 16 inches on center (OC). This means the distance from the center of one stud to the center of the next is 16 inches. The space between studs that are 16 inches OC is 14½ inches. The first and last studs in a wall are exceptions to the rule. The first stud is shifted over ¾ inch as its centerline corresponds with the end of the wall, so its side is flush with the ends of the plates. This makes the space between the first and second studs 13¾ inches.

The last stud in the wall may or may not be spaced evenly. Its position depends on the length of the wall. Thus the spacing between it and the second-to-last stud can be anything from a couple of inches to the standard 14½ inches. Whatever you do, don't adjust the spacing of all the studs to avoid having a single odd space. If you do, the edges of your drywall sheets won't line up with the studs.

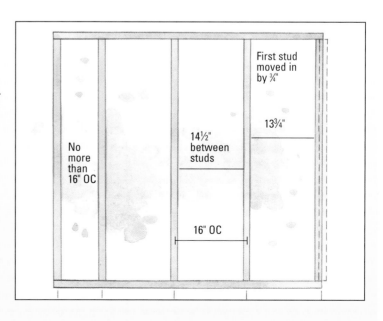

B. Set the wall into position

Once a wall is framed, put it in place as quickly as possible to free up the floor space. Before lifting the wall, double-check to make sure its height matches or is less than the distance from the floor to the underside of the plate that's attached to the ceiling.

Use a plumb bob and a chalk line to locate the position of the bottom plate on the floor. Lift up the wall and slide it into position, then nail it in place.

It's a good idea to have a helper for this part of the job. Otherwise, if the wall is long, you could strain your back or rack the wall. Even if the wall is short enough to raise and move yourself, it's easier to mark for plumb and hold the wall in position for nailing if you have a helper. Besides, you'll only need a hand for a few minutes.

Plumb bob

1 Dangle a plumb bob from the end and side of the ceiling plate to transfer the wall location to the floor. If you are working alone, hang the plumb bob from a nail in the plate. Repeat at the other end. This job is quicker with two people: One holds the string, the other marks the spot.

2 Snap a chalk line between the two marks you located with the plumb bob. This line indicates where the side of the bottom plate will go.

WHAT IF ...
You are anchoring walls to concrete floors?

Setting up a wall on a concrete floor presents a problem—it is difficult to nail into concrete. There are two approaches you can try. The first is to use masonry nails, specially hardened nails designed to be driven into hard masonry materials. You don't have to drive them very deep—½ inch is plenty—so 2-inch nails work well. Concrete continues to harden for years after it is poured, however, so after three or four years it may prove too tough even for masonry nails. Try a couple to see if they go in. The second approach is to glue the bottom plate in place with construction adhesive.

Other methods for attaching framing to concrete include masonry screws and power-actuated fasteners, but these are unnecessary for a wooden partition wall. Nails or adhesive are strong enough to prevent the bottom plate from sliding sideways.

Masonry nails work well to anchor the plate to a slab if the concrete is not too old. Be sure to **wear safety goggles** when hammering nails into concrete.

Construction adhesive is an effective way to secure the bottom plate—it just costs a bit more than masonry nails. The adhesive comes in tubes with tapered nozzles. Cut off the nozzle close enough to the tube to give you a bead that's about ½ inch wide. Use plenty of adhesive.

3 Position the wall so the bottom plate is about a foot away from the chalk line. Lift the wall by the top plate and tip it up until it is vertical. Slide it into position under the ceiling plate.

4 Anchor the wall by nailing up through the top plate into the ceiling plate. Make sure the edges of the two plates are flush. To protect a plaster ceiling, install the plate with 2½-inch-long drywall screws. Check the wall for plumb with a carpenter's level, then nail the bottom plate to the floor.

5 If there is a little space between the top plate and the ceiling plate, slip a pair of shims in between the two before nailing. Drive the nails through the shims to keep them from slipping out.

Framing a corner

If your new wall turns a corner, frame it with four studs or with three studs and blocking as shown here. This creates a sturdy corner that provides a 1-inch-wide nailing surface for inside-corner drywall as well as solid nailing for drywall on the outside corner.

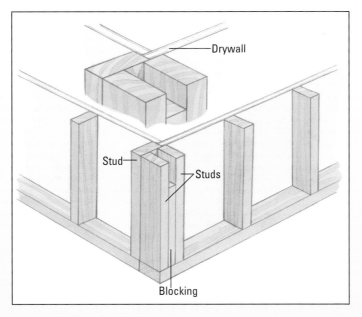

Drywall

Stud

Studs

Blocking

STANLEY PRO TIP

Plumb with a chalk line

If you don't have a plumb bob in your toolbox, use a chalk line instead. The case on most models comes to a point for just this purpose.

FRAMING A DOORWAY

Framing a doorway is similar to framing a solid wall, with a few added elements (see Anatomy of Walls and Ceilings, *page 6*). Like the rest of the wall, it is easier to make a rough opening for a doorway while the wall is flat on the floor, if you have room to work that way. Select the straightest studs you can find for framing doorways; you will avoid problems later.

When you build the wall, the bottom plate runs across the bottom of the doorway. This keeps the entire wall in one plane as you install it. To make it easier to remove the bottom plate under the door, cut most of the way through it in the correct places with a circular saw. Do this before installing the studs, which later won't leave you room to make the cuts with a power saw. After the wall is anchored securely, you can finish the cuts easily with a handsaw and remove the plate from the door opening.

PRESTART CHECKLIST

☐ **TIME**
About 1 hour

☐ **TOOLS**
Tape measure, layout square, circular saw, handsaw, hammer, level

☐ **SKILLS**
Measuring and marking, crosscutting, driving nails

☐ **PREP**
Determine the size of the rough opening

☐ **MATERIALS**
2×4s, 16d nails, 10d nails, 8d nails

Top side of bottom plate

1 Lay out the positions of the jack and king studs on the two plates. Set a circular saw to make a cut 1⅛ inches deep. Cut across the bottom plate to establish the width of the rough opening. Make the cuts on the waste side of the lines marking the sides of the jack studs.

2 The king studs run from plate to plate. Nail them in place as you would regular studs. Cut the jack studs to a length equal to the rough opening height minus 1½ inches to allow for the bottom plate. Nail the jack studs to the bottom plate with 16d nails and to the sides of the king studs with 10d nails.

ROUGH OPENING
Leaving room for more work

When you make a space in a wall for a door or a window, it is called a rough opening. For a door, the rough opening is usually 2 inches wider and taller than the size of the door itself, not including the jambs. This allows space for the jambs plus a little extra for shimming the assembly should the opening not be exactly plumb.

A typical residential door is 32 inches wide and 80 inches tall, so the rough opening is 34 inches wide and 82 inches tall. Rather than rely on these dimensions, however, purchase (or at least measure) the door you will be installing before framing the opening. If you are in doubt about how big to make the opening, make it ¼ inch on the larger side. You can always use shims to make a too-small door fit, but a door that is too big for its opening is a nuisance to cut down. Doors are

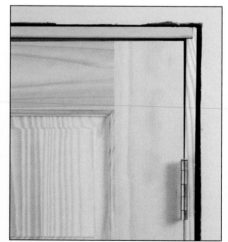

available in many sizes, so if a 32-inch door doesn't work for you, ask your supplier what else is available.

3 In a partition wall, the header for the top of the door opening doesn't bear a load. Make it from doubled 2×4s nailed together with 10d nails. Install the header with two 16d nails through each king stud.

4 Nail one cripple to each king stud with 10d nails to hold the header firmly down on the jack studs. Attach them to the top plate with 16d nails. The infill cripples continue the 16-inch OC spacing of the wall studs regardless of where the door is located. Space the infill cripples accordingly. Attach them with 16d nails through the top plate and 8d toenails into the header. Make sure the sides of the door opening are plumb. Tip the wall into place as described on *pages 54–55*.

Removing the bottom plate

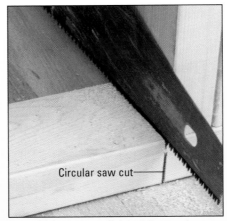

Circular saw cut

After the wall is anchored in place, remove the length of bottom plate that crosses the doorway. Use a handsaw to finish the cuts you started in Step 1. Be careful not to cut into the floor on either side of the doorway.

To avoid damaging a finished floor, make saw cuts (see Step 1) on the underside of the bottom plate instead of the top. This is a little trickier because you have to extend the layout cuts around the plate, cut exactly to the line, and nail the stud exactly in the right spot.

STANLEY PRO TIP

Need an extra set of hands?

When you are trying to tap a wall into position and get it plumb, it can be awkward to hold a level at the same time. Clamp a level to the side of one of the studs for hands-free viewing.

FRAMING WITH METAL

The traditional choice of materials for framing houses is wood. In commercial construction, steel framing is the norm, largely because steel studs are inherently fire-resistant. Steel framing, however, is gradually catching on with home remodelers. It has some real advantages over wood: It is lightweight, inexpensive, and strong. In addition, it won't rot, shrink, or warp (steel framing is ideal for framing walls in a basement, where moisture can create problems).

Walls framed with steel are built in place, one piece at a time. The primary fastener is a sheet metal screw; the primary tools are a drill/driver and metal snips.

PRESTART CHECKLIST

☐ **TIME**
About 1 to 2 hours for a 12-foot wall

☐ **TOOLS**
Tape measure, chalk line, plumb bob, drill/driver, metal snips

☐ **SKILLS**
Measuring and laying out, power-driving screws, cutting sheet metal

☐ **PREP**
Planning where walls are to go

☐ **MATERIALS**
Metal track and studs (4 studs for the first 4 feet of wall, 3 studs for every 4 feet thereafter), pan-head sheet metal screws

SAFETY FIRST
Protect your eyes

It's smart to wear safety goggles or safety glasses whenever you drive fasteners, but especially so when driving fasteners into concrete, which easily chips when hit.

1 Lay out both sides of the wall on the floor with chalk lines. For a concrete floor, predrill ⅛-inch holes and attach the track with concrete screws. Use pan-head sheet metal screws for a wooden floor (see "Fasteners for metal framing" on page 59).

2 Transfer the layout from the floor to the ceiling with a plumb bob. If your wall runs parallel to the joists, install blocking to provide an anchor point (page 51). Screw the track to the joists with pan-head sheet metal screws.

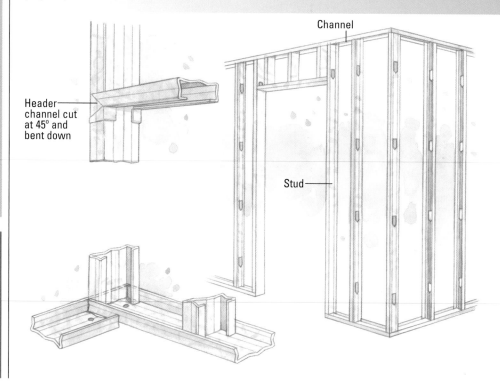

Channel

Header channel cut at 45° and bent down

Stud

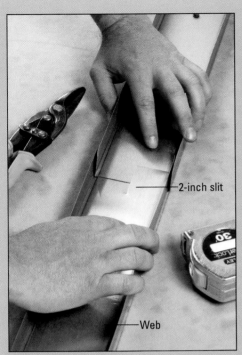

3 To splice two lengths of track together, cut a 2-inch slit in the center of one piece's web. Compress the flanges and slide it into the adjoining piece. For corners, remove the flange from one of the pieces and overlap the webs as shown in the illustration (below left).

4 Lay out the stud locations on the top and bottom tracks. Cut the studs to length and stand them in the tracks. Friction will hold them in place while you check them for plumb. Fasten them with short pan-head sheet metal screws.

5 Make doorway headers from lengths of track. Cut the flanges at 45 degrees and bend down the web to form a right angle. The bent part should be about 1½ to 2 inches long. Attach the header with a single screw driven through each of the four resulting tabs.

Fastening metal framing

Metal framing relies on various kinds of screws. You'll want to stock some of each. One type of screw is a **pan-head sheet metal screw.** For attaching metal pieces together, use screws that are ½ inch long. These same screws can be used for attaching the track to a wooden floor and to the ceiling joists. If the ceiling is already covered with drywall, you'll have to use 1¼-inch-long screws to reach through the drywall into the joists. For attaching drywall to metal studs, 1¼-inch **drywall screws** are in order; for attaching trim, use 1½-inch (or longer) **trim-head screws.** Trim-head screws have small diameter heads that countersink neatly. The resulting holes easily can be filled. Finally, if you have to fasten metal track to a concrete floor, use **power-actuated fasteners** or **concrete screws.** The power-actuated fasteners are fired from a nail gun you can rent. Get a #3 load with a ½- or ⅝- inch pin.

Add plywood blocking

If you will be hanging cabinets or trim on a wall that's framed with metal studs, install pieces of ¾-inch plywood between the studs to provide something to screw into. Likewise you can also insert 2×4s into headers and studs at door openings for attachment of door jambs.

ENLARGING A LOAD-BEARING WALL OPENING

Enlarging an opening between two rooms is a relatively easy and inexpensive way to make a house seem larger without actually adding space. If the opening is in a nonbearing partition wall, the process is straightforward: Simply remove the drywall and reframe the opening to its new size. The size of the header can be a purely aesthetic decision. In fact, you don't need a header at all.

If the wall is a load-bearing wall, however, the process is a little more complicated. You must build temporary walls on both sides of the bearing wall to carry the load while you work on the opening, as described in Step 1. You'll also have to add a larger header (or beam) to carry the load over a wider span. See "Is This Wall Structural?" *(page 10)* to help determine if a wall is load-bearing.

PRESTART CHECKLIST

☐ **TIME**
About 8 to 12 hours to remove wall and replace with new header

☐ **TOOLS**
Tape measure, hammer, circular saw, level, bottle jacks

☐ **SKILLS**
Demolition, cutting pieces to precise lengths, hammering

☐ **PREP**
Planning and calculating the size of the header

☐ **MATERIALS**
Lumber for header and posts, lumber for temporary supports, duplex staging nails, 8d nails, 10d nails, 16d nails

Towels for padding

Supports

1 Strip the drywall or plaster from the wall you want to modify. Locate and count the joists that are supported by the wall. Cut two 2×4 studs for each joist (their length should be the distance from the floor to the ceiling less 3 inches). Have helpers hold a temporary 2×4 plate along the ceiling, 2 feet away from the wall. Protect the ceiling with old towels. Place another plate on the floor and wedge the studs in place between the two plates. The studs should be under the joists. Nail the pieces together with duplex staging nails, which have a double head to make them easy to pull. Repeat on the other side of the wall. Tear out the old wall only after both supports are in place.

Trimming built-up headers and posts

Tripled headers and posts such as the ones used above are 4½ inches thick, 1 inch thicker than the studs. When you attach ½-inch drywall to each side of the studs, the drywall will be in the same plane as the header and posts. Cover the wood-to-drywall joint with wide boards of a nice grade of wood, such as oak. Preassemble the post pieces with glue and clamps to minimize the nail holes you'll need to fill.

Drywall butts into header and posts.

Preassembled post cover

These oak trim boards, prestained and varnished, give the new wall opening a substantial, timber-framed look. Attach the trim with pairs of 8d finishing nails about every 2 feet.

2 Select a header design. To make the 9-foot-long, 4½-inch-thick header shown here, three 2×10s are nailed together with 10d nails.

Bottle jack

Support

3 Prop the new header in place. Use two hydraulic bottle jacks under 4×4 posts to press the header tightly against the joists. Bottle jacks are available at most rental centers. Toe-nail up through the header into the joists.

Tripled 2×6 header

2×4 centered on header

4 Make two posts from two or three 2×4s or 2×6s. In this case, tripled 2×6s are used. Toe-nail them to both the header and the plate. As shown here, a 2×4 is centered on each post. Drywall will abut the posts and be attached to these studs.

HEADER DESIGN
A longer span calls for a stronger beam

Several considerations go into sizing a header. A wider opening, for instance, requires a stronger header, and the length of the joists supported by the header matters too—the longer the joists, the more weight each carries, so longer joists need stronger headers. It also matters whether the new beam will support more than one floor.

Some species of wood are stronger than others. Lumber suppliers provide span tables to help you size beams, but if you are inexperienced, it's best to consult a carpenter or structural engineer.

Depending on your priorities, you have some options when it comes to designing a header. For example, if you have plenty of headroom and want to make the header flush to a 2×4 wall, a header of doubled 2×12s does the job of tripled 2×8s. If headroom is limited and you want a flush header, a steel beam may be the answer.

Other options include glue-laminated and parallel-strand beams, two forms of manufactured lumber that are stronger than sawed lumber.

½-inch plywood

A header constructed of two pieces of 2× lumber with a piece of ½-inch plywood between will create a 3½-inch-thick header that will be flush with the studs.

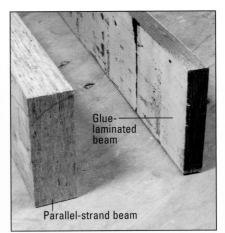

Glue-laminated beam

Parallel-strand beam

Parallel-strand beams consist of strands of wood fiber oriented parallel to their length and bonded with glue. Glue-laminated beams are glued layers of wood.

BUILDING CABINETS INTO A WALL

The space inside the walls of a typical home is underutilized. If you're looking for a place to put a new display cabinet, bookshelf, medicine cabinet, or even an ironing board, consider tapping into this unused real estate. Don't put cabinets in outside walls, though. The gain in storage isn't worth the loss of insulation.

Start by locating the wall's studs, along with any utilities. Then determine if your built-in will fit between the studs (in a wall framed 16 inches OC, the space between the studs is 14½ inches), or whether you will have to rework the framing and possibly reroute some utilities.

PRESTART CHECKLIST

☐ **TIME**
About 1 to 2 hours for a simple cutout; up to 8 hours or more for a cutout that involves cutting studs and reframing

☐ **TOOLS**
Tape measure, framing square, level, jab saw, circular saw, drill/driver, hammer

☐ **SKILLS**
Measuring and laying out, cutting drywall, cutting studs in place, toe-nailing

☐ **PREP**
Locate studs and utilities, determine opening size

☐ **MATERIALS**
Four 6-inch lengths of 2×4, 10d nails, 2½-inch drywall screws, 1¼-inch wood screws

Installing a cabinet between studs

1 A standard medicine cabinet fits between existing studs. Lay out the opening on the wall. Drill holes at the corners to help start the cuts. Saw along the lines with a jab saw.

6-inch-long blocks

Space for header

Space for sill

2 Use 2½-inch drywall screws to attach 6-inch-long blocks to the studs to help position a header and sill in the opening. Use four screws per block and position the blocks 1½ inches from the top and bottom of the opening.

Header

Sill

3 Place the header and sill against the blocks. Attach them at each end with one nail toed into the stud and another hammered down into the block. Install the cabinet with 1¼-inch wood screws.

WHAT IF...
The cabinet is too deep for the wall cavity?

A regular 2×4 stud wall with drywall on either side can accommodate a cabinet that is about 4 inches deep. A wall with plaster and lath can be as much as 1 inch deeper. If you have an even deeper cabinet, allow it to protrude from the wall and use extension pieces to bridge the gap between the wall and the cabinet front. Predrill and screw the pieces to the cabinet or wall.

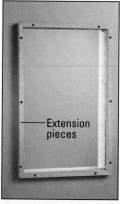

Extension pieces

Installing a cabinet wider than the studs

Unless you limit yourself to small, narrow cabinets placed where studs dictate, you will have to cut away a stud or two to accomplish your plans. If the wall you are cutting into is load-bearing, you'll have to brace the ceiling before you cut *(page 60)* and add a header to distribute the load.

For spans up to 3 feet wide, a double 2×4 header is adequate; for spans from 4 feet to 5 feet, a double 2×6 is required. Make the 2×6 header from two pieces of lumber with ½-inch plywood between to equal the 3½-inch thickness of the wall framing. For walls that don't bear a load, a single 2×4 header is fine.

The cabinet opening shown here is in a bearing wall and requires that two studs be cut. That's a span of about 4 feet, so a doubled 2×6 header is used.

Unlike a cabinet that simply fits between studs *(page 62),* wider cabinets require you to remove drywall beyond the final opening. Patch the areas with new drywall and finish the joints before you install the cabinet. You may also want to paint the new drywall before installing the cabinet.

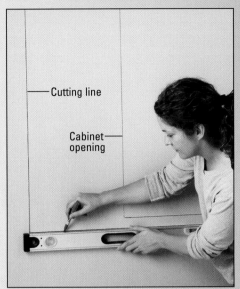

1 Lay out the cabinet opening on the wall. Then lay out the cut lines around the cabinet outline. You'll need to allow 1½ inches for a sill underneath and, in this case, 5½ inches for a header above. The side cut lines appear along the inside edges of the nearest studs. Cut along the lines with a jab saw or other handsaw.

2 If you are cutting into a bearing wall, construct bracing on both sides of the wall as shown on *pages 60–61.* Cut through the necessary studs that are even with the opening. Start the cuts with a circular saw; finish with a handsaw. Be careful not to damage the drywall at the rear of the cavity.

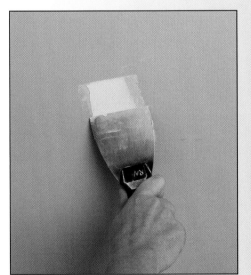

3 After the studs are cut, they will still be attached to the drywall on the opposite side of the wall. Pry them out; you will probably damage the drywall on the back of the opening as the fasteners pull through. To patch the holes, see Repairing Drywall on *page 80.*

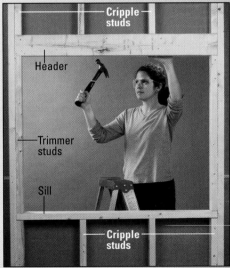

4 Nail four new cripple studs to the inside faces of the full studs: two at the top and two at the bottom. Nail the sill in place. Add trimmer studs on both sides of the opening and a header across the top. Toe-nail up through the outside face of the header to catch the bottoms of the cripples.

5 Cut spacer blocks to position the cripple jack studs that will make the sides of the opening. Nail the spacers in place to the sill and header, then nail the cripples to the spacers. Make the opening ¼ inch wider than the intended cabinet. Install drywall to close in the rest of the wall *(pages 68–79).*

INSULATING A WALL

Insulation helps control a room's climate, in terms of both temperature and noise level. For basement walls, especially masonry walls, rigid foam is an ideal insulator because it is unaffected by moisture and water.

One option is to attach furring strips to the walls and to glue foam insulation between them. Another, better way is to install 2-foot-wide foam board with steel Z-channels. This eliminates the need for glue and virtually eliminates the loss of insulation value that occurs with furring strips. Rent a power-actuated nailer to attach the channels to masonry. This tool uses a small gunpowder charge to drive in fasteners. To install drywall, drive drywall screws right through the Z-channels.

Insulate interior walls for sound control. If you have room for slightly thicker walls, add significant soundproofing by weaving batts of insulation between studs *(page 65)*.

PRESTART CHECKLIST

☐ **TIME**
Fiberglass insulation: ½ to 1 hour for an 8-foot wall; rigid foam insulation: ½ to 1 hour for a 12-foot wall

☐ **TOOLS**
Batts: scissors and staple gun
Rigid foam: serrated kitchen knife, power-actuated nail gun, utility knife, tape measure

☐ **SKILLS**
Stapling, cutting thick material

☐ **PREP**
For fiberglass insulation, wall should be framed; utilities installed

☐ **MATERIALS**
Fiberglass insulation batts, ¼-inch staples; for rigid foam insulation, power-actuated fasteners (#3 load, ½-inch pin)

Fiberglass rolls and batts

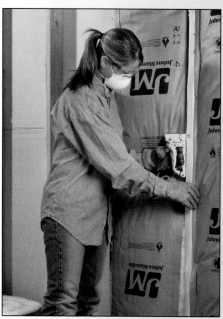

Fiberglass insulation comes sized to fit between studs that are either 16 or 24 inches on center. You can buy it in rolls or in batts that are precut to the length of stud bays. For sound control, the paper facing is not necessary but provides a convenient flap for stapling.

To fit the insulation into narrow or irregularly shaped spaces, cut the batt with a pair of scissors. Cut the piece a little oversized, then fold back the paper to use as a stapling flange. Don't cram the material into spaces; it loses its insulating value when compressed.

STANLEY PRO TIP

The well-dressed insulater

Installing insulation can be itchy business. Dress properly for the job to avoid discomfort. Wear long pants and a long-sleeve shirt, buttoned up to the collar and at the sleeves. Wear a dust mask specifically designed to be effective for fiberglass insulation. Gloves reduce the itch, but they make handling the necessary tools a bit awkward. When you are finished, shower first with cold water; it closes your pores to reduce itch. Wash your insulating work clothes separately in hot water on an extended wash cycle.

Some fiberglass insulation is designed to be less itchy. One style wraps each batt or roll in its own plastic sack. Another uses fibers that are curly and therefore less irritating.

Facing in the right direction

If you are installing fiberglass insulation in outside walls, you need to pay attention to the paper facing. The facing is a vapor retarder, meant to slow the migration of water vapor through the wall. If warm, moist air from inside a house travels through the wall, it will condense when it hits the cold sheathing on the outside. If the sheathing is damp from condensation, it eventually wets the insulation, decreasing its effectiveness. Damp sheathing is also prone to rot. If the outside air is warm and the inside air is cool, the process works in reverse, causing condensation on the drywall. If you live in a climate where you heat in the winter, place the paper toward the inside of the house. If you live where air-conditioning is used more often than heat, face the paper to the outside.

Rigid foam on masonry walls

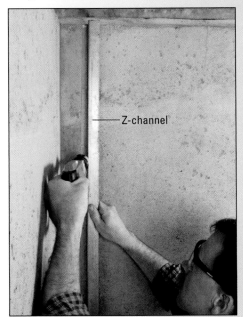

1 Install a piece of Z-channel in one corner, with the flange facing the wall. Leave enough room for a piece of foam and a piece of drywall along the adjacent wall. Attach the channel with power-actuated fasteners. Use a #3 load with a ½-inch pin, five per channel.

2 Slip a piece of foam under the Z-channel and trap it in place with a second piece of channel on the other side, its flange pointing in the opposite direction. The channels have a slight angle built into them that grips the insulation. Continue this pattern until you reach the next corner.

3 When you reach the second corner, cut the last piece of foam (use a serrated kitchen knife) so the final Z-channel fits into the corner, leaving enough room for a piece of foam and a piece of drywall on the adjacent wall. Start the adjacent wall by slipping insulation into the gap you left.

Adding soundproofing with fiberglass batts

1 Use 2×6s for the top and bottom plates and end studs, 2×4s for the rest of the studs. Build the wall on the floor *(page 52–53)*. Mark the plates for studs 8 inches on center (OC) to provide 16-inch OC nailing on each side of the wall. Install the studs that are flush to one side of the plates. If you have room, flip over the wall and install the remaining studs; otherwise, tip the wall into position, then install the rest of the studs.

2 Weave a continuous roll of fiberglass insulation between the staggered studs, using insulation designed for 2×4 walls. Weave loosely to fill the cavity but tightly enough so you won't have to compress the insulation when you install drywall. When you reach the end of the wall, cut off the insulation. Weave additional lengths of insulation in the same manner on top of each other until you fill the wall to the top.

COVERING WALLS & CEILINGS

With the framing in place, it is time to call in the professionals or do your own utility work in the open walls. Look for *Stanley Advanced Wiring* and *Stanley Advanced Plumbing* for complete how-to information on those subjects. Once the utilities are roughed in, you can tackle the next phase of the project: closing in the walls and ceilings.

Today the vast majority of new walls and ceilings are made with drywall, also known as gypsum board, wallboard, plasterboard, or by the brand name Sheetrock. Even if you are planning a different finished wall surface, such as paneling or tile, your local building codes likely require drywall or plaster underneath to provide fire protection.

Drywall is the most commonly used material for good reason. It is fire-resistant, relatively inexpensive, reasonably easy to install, and provides a smooth, flat surface that is easy to paint.

Get help with the hanging

The key to hanging drywall with a minimum of fuss is to get some help. Drywall sheets are heavy and awkward; having someone to help move and hang them more than doubles your efficiency—even if your helper has few tool skills—and saves you from sore muscles.

Even if you have a helper, consider renting a drywall lift *(page 73)*, especially if you have a lot of ceiling pieces to install. This back-saving tool holds a sheet of drywall; when you turn a crank, it hoists the sheet up to the ceiling or wall.

Finishing with finesse

Finishing the joints between drywall sheets takes more skill than muscle. An experienced drywall finisher can quickly make seams that disappear under a coat of paint. It may take a do-it-yourselfer longer at first, but you can always improve a joint with a little more joint compound or a little more sanding. With patience you can achieve professional-quality results.

A little help and a lot of patience are the keys to pro-quality drywall work.

CHAPTER PREVIEW

Hanging drywall
page 68

Creating an arched passageway
page 74

Finishing drywall
page 76

Repairing drywall
page 80

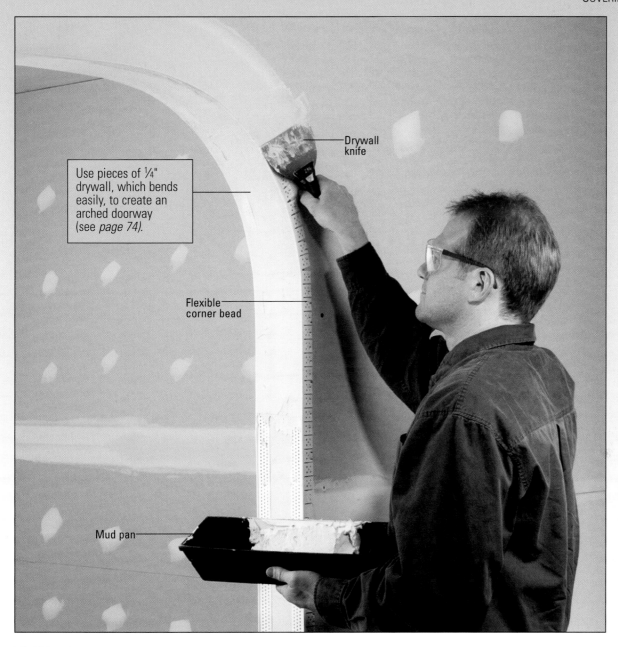

Use pieces of ¼" drywall, which bends easily, to create an arched doorway (see *page 74*).

Drywall knife

Flexible corner bead

Mud pan

With some patient work and attention to detail, you can create a smooth, seamless wall surface ready for paint or wallpaper.

Repairing plaster
page 82

Installing a dropped ceiling
page 84

HANGING DRYWALL

You can use nails or screws to attach drywall to the framing. Nailing is the fastest method, but nails sometimes pop out later, creating small bumps on the wall surface. (Nail pops occur when studs dry, forcing nails out a little, or if the drywall wasn't nailed tightly to begin with.) Screws cost a bit more in time and money, but they rarely produce pops. Screws must be used when working with steel studs.

Another option is to hold the drywall in place with construction adhesive. This allows you to use fewer nails or screws, reducing the time needed to fill fastener dimples. Adhesive also makes a stiffer wall and reduces nail pops.

You must also decide whether to attach the rectangular sheets horizontally or vertically. Most drywall installers prefer to run the sheets horizontally, which makes for a stronger wall, especially if you're working with steel studs. In addition it places long joints about 4 feet up from the floor, a convenient height for finishing. Stagger the vertical seams if you can—doing so makes the wall stronger.

PRESTART CHECKLIST

☐ **TIME**
About 15 to 30 minutes per sheet of drywall, depending on the complexity of the shape

☐ **TOOLS**
Tape measure, chalk line, screw gun or hammer, drywall T-square, utility knife

☐ **SKILLS**
Measuring and laying out, driving screws or nails, cutting with a utility knife

☐ **PREP**
Framing completed, utilities in place

☐ **MATERIALS**
Drywall sheets, 1¼-inch drywall nails or screws

Hanging horizontal pieces

1 Screw a 2×2 ledger about 52 inches below the ceiling. Place the drywall on the ledger. Make sure the sheet ends on the middle of a stud; if it doesn't, cut it. Mark the stud locations and snap chalk lines. Then push up the sheet tight against the ceiling and fasten it.

2 Cut the bottom piece about 1 inch narrower than the space below the top sheet. With the uncut edge up, pry the sheet tight to the edge of the upper piece and fasten. When installed later, baseboard will hide the gap and the cut edge.

DRYWALL APPLICATION

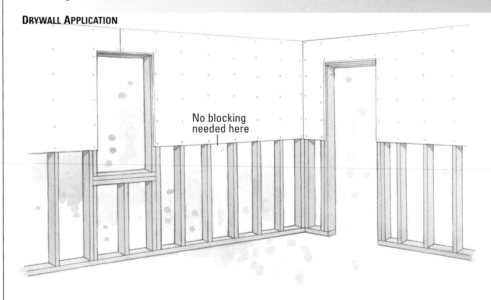

No blocking needed here

In general make as few seams as possible. For example, if you are working on 9-foot walls, use 9-foot sheets hung vertically to avoid having a seam 1 foot from the floor (which would occur with two 4-foot-wide sheets hung horizontally). Joints between horizontal drywall sheets do not require blocking if the studs are not more than 16 inches on center (as shown above).

Cutting drywall

1 Mark the piece about ¼ inch smaller than the space it needs to fit. Use a utility knife to cut through the outside face of the drywall and into the gypsum. Make two or three passes to deepen the cut; you do not need to cut through the sheet.

2 To complete the cut, bump the back of the sheet at the cut line with your knee as you hold the sheet. This will snap the gypsum so you can fold back the sheet. Slice the back paper along the fold line with a utility knife.

Fastening the drywall

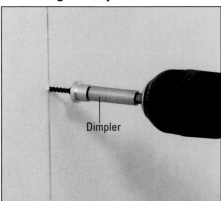

Dimpler

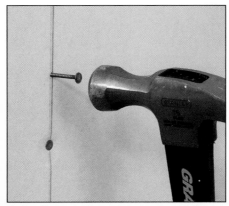

Screws: Use a screw gun with an adjustable clutch or a regular drill with a dimpler attachment. Both the clutch and the dimpler are designed to drive screws so they sink just below the surface without breaking the paper. Space the screws 12 inches apart.

Nails: Double-nail to prevent nail pops. Space drywall nails 12 inches apart, with a second set about 2 inches from the first. Along the edges use single nails 8 inches apart. When a nail is flush to the surface, hit it one more time to create a slight depression, but don't break the paper surface.

Glue: Apply a bead of drywall mastic to each stud. Drive nails or screws into the sheet to hold it in place while the adhesive sets up. You can space the fasteners 18 to 24 inches apart as long as the drywall is held firmly against the studs.

Making cutouts

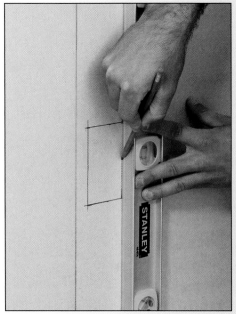

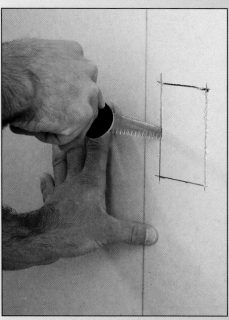

1 To fit drywall over electrical boxes and around other obstacles in the wall, make cutouts for them. Start by measuring and carefully laying out the positions of the cutouts on the face of the sheet.

2 Use a jab saw to make the cutout. To make starting the cut a little easier, drill holes in the corners of the cutout.

3 If you need to trim the opening a little bit to make it fit, use a Surform® plane. Drywall is hard on edge tools, so use one plane or rasp for drywall work and another for shaping wood.

STANLEY PRO TIP

What's in the wall?

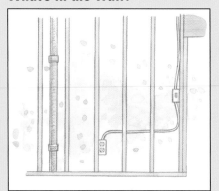

Before closing in the walls, make a diagram noting where the studs fall and the location of anything in the wall, such as wires and pipes. Take a photograph or two as a supplement to the drawings. File them all away for future reference.

WHAT IF...
You have to cut drywall around a window or doorway?

If the wall you are covering includes a door or window opening, run the drywall right over the opening and cut it out after the drywall is fastened in place. If the sheet ends over the opening (as shown above), cut the drywall away with a handsaw, guiding the saw against the framing. It doesn't matter if the cuts are ragged or a little uneven since they will be covered by trim or corner bead.

If the drywall runs completely over the top of the doorway, use a handsaw to cut along the jack studs until you reach the bottom of the header on both sides. Snap a chalk line to mark the bottom of the header and cut along the line with your utility knife. Snap back the waste piece and cut the back paper free.

Applying corner bead

After all the drywall is up, the next step is to apply corner bead. The bead serves two purposes: It protects the corner from impacts, and it provides a guide for your knife as you apply joint compound to the corner. You won't need bead in corners that will receive molding because the molding provides protection and joint compound won't be used on those corners.

There are two styles of bead: standard, which makes a crisp, square corner; and rounded, which makes a softer, smoother corner. Both are available in white vinyl and galvanized steel. Both materials work well, so choose based on price and availability.

You'll need flexible bead to create an arched passageway *(page 74)* or other curves. Flexible bead is similar to standard corner bead but it has cuts across the flanges at regular intervals allowing the bead to bend around a curve.

Whichever type of bead you use, it is better to attach the flanges with drywall nails than with screws, which tend to make the bead pucker. Use nails that penetrate studs or other framing at least ½ inch.

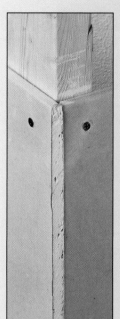

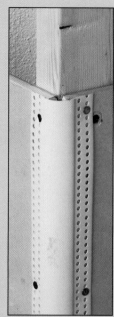
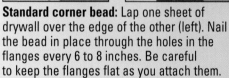

Standard corner bead: Lap one sheet of drywall over the edge of the other (left). Nail the bead in place through the holes in the flanges every 6 to 8 inches. Be careful to keep the flanges flat as you attach them.

Rounded corner bead: This style of corner bead is available in different radii, including some that call for overlapping drywall edges. In most cases though, you'll need to attach the drywall even with the edges of the stud as shown above (left). Then nail the bead every 6 to 8 inches.

STANLEY PRO TIP

Cut corner bead to length

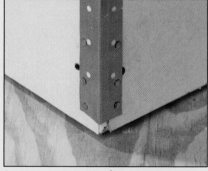

Cut corner bead about ¼ inch short of the corner's height. This makes it easier to put the bead in place. Hold the bead tight to the ceiling as you nail it in place. The baseboard will cover the gap. Drive an extra nail or two at the bottom to reinforce the corner against inevitable kicks and bumps.

WHAT IF...
You have to run drywall up against a post or other surface?

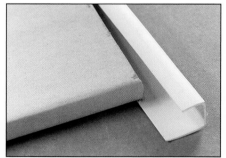

When the raw edge of a piece of drywall meets a dissimilar surface, such as wood, it is nearly impossible to get a clean fit. Two products create a crisp edge in this situation: J-bead (left) is nailed in place on the wall before the drywall is installed. You probably will want to prepaint it, because it remains visible when the job is finished. (Spray paint works well.) J-bead is particularly useful

where condensation might wick into the drywall, spoiling a smooth finishing job. It encases the drywall, isolating it from the abutting material.

L-bead (right) is nailed to the face of the drywall. It will be covered with joint compound (like corner bead) and painted along with the rest of the wall.

Drywall without trim

Entryways and windows in many modern homes are finished with drywall edges instead of wood casings and jambs. Finishing drywall edges takes about the same amount of time as applying trim but saves the cost of the wood pieces.

To trim an entryway, cover the inside surfaces of the jack studs and the bottom of the header with drywall, then finish the corners with corner bead.

For windows, create drywall jamb extensions that fill the space between the edge of the window frame and the surface of the wall. In this application, use J-bead *(page 71)* to encase the drywall edge that abuts the window. The J-bead creates a smooth and straight finished edge. More importantly, it prevents condensation on the window from wicking into the exposed gypsum at the drywall edge.

Note that this treatment won't work with windows that have frames that take up the entire depth of the opening.

J-bead

1 Spray-paint the J-bead before installing it. When the paint is dry, nail strips of J-bead to the jack studs and header, tight against the window frame. If you plan to use drywall at the bottom of the window (rather than a stool), install J-bead there as well.

Surform® plane

2 Slip drywall into the J-bead on the sides and across the top of the window (and the bottom if needed). Plane the edges flush to the wall with a Surform® plane. Nail corner bead around the three corners.

STANLEY PRO TIP

Scribing drywall to fit

To cut a piece of drywall to fit against an irregular surface, hold the piece near the surface and trace the outline onto the sheet with a scribing tool.

Fitting angled pieces

1 Rather than measuring the angle at which a piece must be cut, measure the length of the horizontal rise and the vertical run.

2 Transfer the measurements to the drywall, then draw a cut line between the two marks. Cut and snap the piece along the line.

Hanging drywall on a ceiling

1 In a ceiling, all edges of the drywall should be supported by framing, so you must add blocking between the joists. A 2×3 or a 2×4 attached with its wider side facing down makes a good target for fasteners.

2 Snap chalk lines or draw the location of the joists on the sheets before you hoist them into position. Use ⅝-inch drywall if the joists are more than 16 inches OC. Many drywall T squares have holes in their blades to ease marking. If yours doesn't, drill some on 16-inch (or as needed) centers.

3 Make a pair of deadman braces from 2×4s to help hold the sheets against the ceiling as you work. The length of the legs should be 1 inch more than the floor-to-ceiling height. This allows the braces to be wedged into position.

Using long sheets

Drywall comes in 4×9-foot, 4×10-foot, and 4×12-foot pieces, as well as the standard 4×8 sheet. These larger sizes can make your project easier. For example, if you have a room that is 12 feet wide, use 12-foot sheets for two walls and the ceiling, to avoid butt (end-to-end) joints, which are more difficult to tape and fill.

Before you decide to use long sheets, make sure you will be able to maneuver them through your home and into the work area.

It's a good idea to have two helpers on hand when you install long sheets. The sheets are awkward and heavy, and they may break under their own weight if not properly supported, especially when being raised to a ceiling.

Fixing a cracked plaster ceiling with drywall

Adding a layer of ⅜-inch drywall is an excellent way to restore a cracked or discolored plaster ceiling. Poke nails through the old ceiling until you locate all the joists (work carefully, there may be pipes or wires present), then snap lines along their length. Apply construction adhesive to the back of the sheet. Use about half a tube of adhesive per sheet, applying it in S-shape beads about a foot apart. Fasten with 2½-inch drywall screws into the joists.

Rent a drywall lift —you'll be amazed at how easy it makes the job of drywalling a ceiling, even if you are using 12-foot pieces.

CREATING AN ARCHED PASSAGEWAY

Drywall does more than create flat walls. It is also used to form curves, such as those necessary for an arched entryway. Depending on the width and height of the passageway, you can create a complete arch, where the curves meet in the middle, or an arch with a flat run on the ceiling between the curves.

First, make a full-size cardboard mock-up to simulate the arch in place. This gives you a good idea of how it will look and how much headroom it will provide. The arch itself will be made from plywood ribs with two layers of thin drywall bent over them.

Finishing an arched opening is also quite easy thanks to flexible archway bead. Once the bead is attached, apply joint compound just as you would for any corner bead.

PRESTART CHECKLIST

☐ **TIME**
About 4 hours to complete a single archway

☐ **TOOLS**
Tape measure, jigsaw, drill/driver, hammer

☐ **SKILLS**
Measuring and laying out, cutting with a circular saw, driving screws, hammering nails

☐ **PREP**
Frame the archway

☐ **MATERIALS**
¾-inch plywood, 1×3, ¼-inch drywall, drywall screws, drywall nails, flexible archway bead

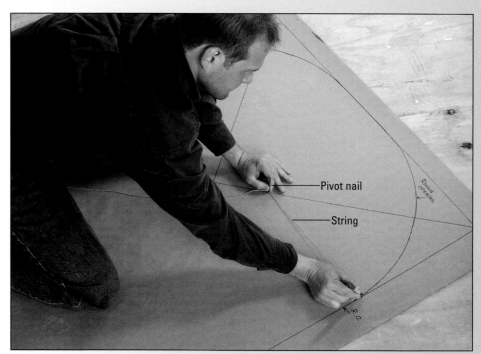

Pivot nail

String

1 Make a full-size drawing of the entry so you can lay out the exact shape and size of the curves. Start with an outline of the rough opening. Draw a line at a 45-degree angle from each corner. The center of the curve will fall along this line. Make a compass using a nail, a string, and a pencil. Draw the curve that represents the finished surface of the drywall. This also will be the curve you cut on the plywood ribs.

STANLEY PRO TIP: **How far will drywall bend?**

Regular ¼-inch drywall can be bent to a curve with a radius of 5 feet. This means the string on your string-and-pencil compass must be at least 5 feet long. For radii of 32 inches or less, purchase ¼-inch drywall that's made specifically for bending. It's usually marked "flexible." If you wet the paper of flexible drywall with a sponge, you can bend it to a radius as small as 20 inches. You don't have to limit yourself to curves governed by a specific radius. If you find a pleasing curve, trace it onto your full-size drawing.

2 Make a pattern by carefully cutting out the curved corner you drew on the cardboard. Use the pattern to lay out the curves on a piece of ¾-inch plywood. Cut four curved ribs with a jigsaw equipped with a fine-tooth blade.

3 Rip-cut four pieces of 1× stock to 2 inches wide to make nailers for the plywood ribs. Make them short enough so their sides will be completely covered by the ribs. Place the nailers in the corners of the doorway and center them from side to side using a scrap of ¾-inch plywood as a guide.

4 Screw the nailers to the corners of the doorway with 1⅝-inch drywall screws. Start the screws in the plywood ribs before you put up the ribs to make them easier to attach to the nailers.

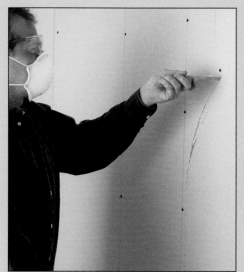

5 Hang the drywall over the arched doorway, just as you would for an ordinary opening. Use a regular handsaw to cut along the jack studs until you reach the curve. Then use a jab saw to cut the curve.

6 Bend a layer of ¼-inch drywall into the curve and fasten it with screws. Bend a second layer over the first and screw it in place as well.

7 Attach drywall to the bottom of the headers and the insides of the jack studs. Use two layers of the same thickness you used for the arch. Attach flexible archway bead to the arched area with drywall nails driven every 6 to 8 inches.

FINISHING DRYWALL

Finishing drywall involves spreading joint compound over the screw or nail holes and joints in the wall to create a smooth, flawless surface. Tape is embedded in the compound over the joints to prevent cracks. The tools and techniques are simple, but creating a smooth surface requires lots of practice. A good pro can finish a wall with three coats, but beginners sometimes need to apply more. You'll need three drywall knives: a 6-inch-wide knife for the first coat, a 10-inch for the second coat, and a 12-inch for the final coat or coats. The three knives allow you to feather out the joint—make it gradually thinner toward the edges so it blends in with the wall surface when painted.

The joint compound used to finish drywall joints is commonly called mud. Use ready-mixed joint compound that comes in 5-gallon buckets. Lesser quantities are available for small jobs. Keep the bucket covered at all times to keep the mud from drying out. Stir in any water that pools on the surface.

PRESTART CHECKLIST

☐ **TIME**
For an 8×8-foot wall, about 1½ hours for the first coat, 45 minutes for each subsequent coat

☐ **TOOLS**
Mud pan; 6-inch, 10-inch, and 12-inch drywall knives; sanding block or sponge

☐ **SKILLS**
Spreading and smoothing joint compound

☐ **PREP**
Check over wall to make sure all fasteners are sunk below surface

☐ **MATERIALS**
Joint compound, fiberglass mesh tape, abrasives

1 Load some joint compound into a mud pan using a 6-inch drywall knife. Start filling the screw or nail dimples with a sweeping motion. Scrape the mud off so the dimple around the screw is filled flush to the surface. Closely spaced dimples can be filled or scraped in one motion.

2 Use fiberglass mesh tape on joints where two tapered edges come together. This self-adhesive mesh costs a little more than paper tape, but it is easier to use and prevents air bubbles. Start at one end and stick the tape in place evenly across the joint along its length.

Sponging to smooth a surface

After you apply the final coat of mud and it dries, the final step is to smooth the surface. You have two choices: sponging or sanding. Each method has its advantage. Sponging avoids creating dust, but sanding does a better job of making the joint flat.

To sponge, you'll need a bucket of water and a big sponge. Even better is a sponge made especially for smoothing drywall; it has a coarse mesh on one side that removes excess mud, and a plain sponge on the opposite side for refining the surface. Wet the sponge and scrub the wall surface. Rinse the sponge frequently to get rid of the mud that builds up on its surface.

Scrape off the ridges and lumps, then sponge the wall smooth. Be careful not to scrub too hard on the paper areas—you can actually wear the paper away and create a rough spot.

3 Cover the tape with a coat of joint compound applied with a 6-inch drywall knife. Scrape it off so the mesh pattern is revealed. Resist the temptation to apply a thick coat—thick applications are hard to keep flat and crack as they dry.

4 There is no need to sand between the first and second coats. Just scrape the ridges and blobs away with your knife after each coat has dried for 24 hours.

5 Apply the second coat with a 10-inch knife. After the coat dries, scrape the high spots and apply the third coat with a 12-inch knife as shown above. Try to feather out the edges of the mud as thinly and smoothly as possible.

Sanding a wall smooth

For an especially smooth, flat joint, you can't beat hand sanding. This method creates lots of dust, but the results are worth it. Be sure to seal off your work area with plastic sheeting *(pages 38–39)* and wear a quality mask to avoid breathing the dust. You might be tempted to use a power sander, but don't. Power sanders fray the drywall's paper and throw large amounts of dust into the air.

For small jobs, a sanding block with regular sandpaper works well. For larger jobs, invest in a sanding screen (a screen mesh impregnated with abrasive) and a holder. Some holders attach to a shop vacuum hose, a setup that helps contain dust during sanding.

Scrape the high spots, then scrub down the wall with a sanding screen. Safety gear is in order, including goggles, dust mask, and ear protectors (because of the vacuum's noise).

STANLEY PRO TIP

Use a pole sander

The universal pole sander extends your reach and allows you to work efficiently by making long strokes. Its name comes from the universal joint that attaches the pole to a sanding pad. This joint ensures that the pad is always flat on the wall. The pad is sized for a half-sheet of sandpaper or a standard sanding screen and has clamps to hold the paper or screen in place.

Finishing butt joints

The long edges of drywall sheets are tapered. Two tapered edges together form a depression, which makes it possible to create a flat mud joint. The short edges of drywall sheets are not tapered; they meet at a butt joint.

Butt joints are more challenging to finish because they require that you build a slight, gradual mound to hide the joint. To make the mound subtle enough to go unnoticed, you must feather the joint compound over a wide area.

The same self-adhesive mesh tape and similar techniques for applying mud are used for butt joints and tapered edges.

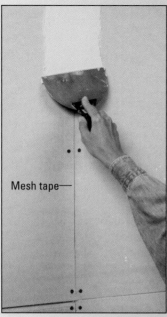

Mesh tape—

1 Cover the butt joint with self-adhesive mesh tape. Use your 6-inch knife to cover the tape with mud.

2 When the first coat of mud is dry, apply the second coat along both sides of the joint using a 6-inch drywall knife.

3 Apply the third coat with a 12-inch drywall knife, feathering the edges out 8 to 10 inches on each side of the joint. You may leave a ridge down the center which can be scraped away later.

STANLEY PRO TIP: **Check the "show coat"**

A work light held at a raking angle helps reveal ridges, bumps, and depressions as you scrape and sand between coats. But your best—and last—chance to fix finish flaws is after you have applied a primer "show coat" to the walls. At this point the walls are a uniform color, and you'll see irregularities you might not have noticed before priming. The most common beginner's mistake is joints that are too thick. If you find joints like this, add another coat of mud and feather it out farther. Sand these joints again, apply primer to any bare mud, and you are ready to apply paint.

SECOND COAT
Try a drywall trowel

If your project includes several butt joints, consider investing in a drywall trowel. It looks like an ordinary mason's trowel, but the blade has an extremely subtle bow that is ideal for forming the slight mound needed for butt joints. Use the trowel for the second coat only, running it once over the center of the joint.

Finishing corners

Covering corner bead at <u>outside corners</u> is easy because the bead itself guides the drywall knife. Run one side of your knife along the bead to produce a smooth, flat joint as the mud covers the nailing flange. As with other joints, apply at least three coats, sanding in between to feather the joint where it meets the drywall. The bead itself isn't hidden in mud. Simply scrape excess mud off the bead, then paint it along with the drywall.

Inside corners are more difficult. They require taping and mudding. The hard part is smoothing the mud on one side of the corner without messing up the mud on the other side.

Resist the temptation to try to get these inside joints perfect on the first, or even second, coat. Accept that there will be ridges you'll need to sand or knock off in the first two coats. To avoid ridges on the third coat, think of it as a "fill" coat; press hard on the knife so you fill imperfections instead of leaving behind a thick layer of joint compound. Remember there's no law against hitting the joints a fourth time if necessary for a smooth finish.

Finishing inside corners

1 Apply mud to both sides of the corner. Fold a length of paper tape in half (it is precreased) and press it into the mud with a 6-inch knife. Don't use mesh tape for corners; it's not strong enough.

2 Bed the tape in the mud by drawing down the knife along both sides of the corner. Repeat this process to apply additional coats of mud. Sand to smooth the final surface.

OUTSIDE CORNERS
Let the bead be your guide

For outside corners, mud the flanges of the corner bead. Apply several coats, sanding the final coat for a smooth surface.

WHAT IF ...
There are bubbles under the paper tape?

If there are bubbles under the tape, the tape doesn't stick to the mud, or it wrinkles, peel it off and apply more mud underneath. This is one time when applying a little too much mud is not a problem.

STANLEY PRO TIP
Consider using a corner knife

One way to achieve straight, smooth inside corners is to use a corner knife. First embed and cover the tape in mud using a 6-inch knife, but don't try to smooth the joint. Next hold the corner knife at the top of the joint, angling it slightly away from the wall, and pull it down to near the floor. Try to do this in one even stroke. The corner knife leaves ridges on both sides of the joint. When dry, scrape off the ridges before you apply a second coat.

REPAIRING DRYWALL

In every remodeling job, some drywall repair work inevitably must be done. You may need to patch a hole left from moving an electrical receptacle or a wall damaged as you moved materials.

Keep track of damage as the job progresses, then tackle the repairs as you tape and mud the new work.

While small dings or hairline cracks in the drywall can simply be filled with joint compound, cracks wider than about $\frac{1}{16}$ inch should be covered with tape before they're filled. Small holes can be covered with a piece of joint tape, then filled with compound. But if the hole is any larger than about 1 inch, you'll need to install a patch of drywall with tape to reinforce the joints between the wall and the patches.

The easiest material to use is self-adhering fiberglass mesh tape. This is applied to the bare drywall, then covered with mud. Because it doesn't require a bed of mud, patches made with mesh tape are thinner than those made with paper tape and easier to blend into the wall.

PRESTART CHECKLIST

☐ **TIME**
About an hour to patch a hole and apply the first coat of mud; then several 20-minute sessions to apply additional coats

☐ **TOOLS**
Utility knife, jab saw, 6-inch drywall knife, abrasive paper, drill/driver

☐ **SKILLS**
Cutting drywall, driving screws, applying joint compound, sanding

☐ **PREP**
Spread drop cloths if patches are done over finished flooring/carpeting

☐ **MATERIALS**
Drywall, drywall screws joint compound, wood scraps, mesh tape

Repairing dings

1 Small dings and minor scuffs are easy to repair. Cut away the damaged paper and loose gypsum with a utility knife.

2 Apply joint compound to the area with a swiping motion. Try to fill the ding without leaving a lot of mud on the surrounding area. Two or more coats may be necessary. Sand the final coat smooth and paint to match the wall.

STANLEY PRO TIP: **Use setting-type joint compound for strength**

Two types of joint compound are available. Ready-mix, which comes premixed in buckets, is easier to apply and sand, but isn't as strong as powder. It can be softened with water after it cures, giving you the option of smoothing it with a sponge instead of abrasive paper.

The other formula is setting-type joint compound, which comes as a powder that must be mixed with water. The bag it comes in is labeled "90," "45," or "20." The numbers indicate how many minutes it takes for the compound to set up. The safest approach is to use the 90-minute mix. If you want it to set faster, mix it with warm water.

Once set, setting-type compound cannot be softened with water. It is harder to sand flat than ready-mix but much stronger. Professional drywall finishers often use

setting-type for the first coat of mud, especially at outside corners, which are vulnerable to damage. It is also useful when patching drywall, as it helps reinforce the repair. Because this compound sets up so fast, you may be able to apply two or more coats in a day.

When you mix setting-type joint compound, mix only what you can use in the time indicated on the label. Otherwise the compound will set before you can apply it. Be sure to use clean water and a clean bucket. Pouring water into the fine powder raises a lot of dust, so put the proper amount of water in the bucket first, then add mix, stirring as you go until you reach a consistency that spreads easily but sticks to the drywall without running. You can always add a little water to the power.

Patching a hole

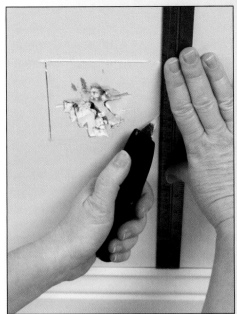

Temporary long screw in 1×3
to grip while driving screws

1 Use a straightedge and utility knife to square the opening. Slide a length or two of scrap 1×3 into the opening. The piece(s) should extend several inches beyond the edges of the hole at both sides.

2 Screw the 1×3(s) to the back of the wall surrounding the hole with 1¼-inch drywall screws. Drive the screws in deep enough that their heads are below the surface but not so deep that they break the drywall's paper face.

3 Cut a patch to fit the opening using drywall of the same thickness as the wall. It doesn't have to fit precisely. Gaps up to ¼ inch are acceptable because they will be filled by tape and compound. Attach the patch to the 1×3(s) with drywall screws.

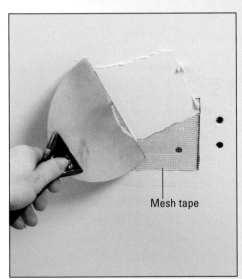

Mesh tape

4 Tape over the joints with fiberglass mesh tape. Spread mud over the tape and screw holes.

5 Scrape away the high spots and apply a second and third coat of mud to the patch. Shine a light across the surface at a raking angle to reveal bumps and depressions. Sand smooth. Apply more mud if necessary.

Patching cracks

Cracks in drywall most often occur at joints when the framing shrinks, creating a slight gap between the drywall sheets. If the crack is a hairline, simply fill it with compound. If it is wider than about ¹⁄₁₆ inch, span the crack with mesh tape, then apply several coats of mud just as you would for a new joint. Sand between the coats as needed.

REPAIRING PLASTER

The task of repairing plaster walls and ceilings is similar to repairing drywall, especially in regard to the materials used. However, the techniques differ somewhat because the wall or ceiling is assembled differently. Plaster is applied as a wet mix over material called lath. In older houses, the lath usually consists of a series of thin slats of wood nailed to the studs. As the plaster is applied, it oozes through the gaps in the lath and forms "keys," which hold the plaster to the wall. Modern plaster uses expanded metal mesh in place of wooden slats. Occasionally you may find plaster that has been spread over a material called gypsum lath.

Plaster can fail in several ways. As a house ages and settles, the movement causes plaster walls to crack. Direct blows punch holes in a wall or cause plaster to come loose; water damage does the same thing. Excessive vibration, such as that caused by heavy truck traffic on a nearby road, can cause large sections of plaster to come loose from its lath.

PRESTART CHECKLIST

☐ **TIME**
About 45 minutes for a hole

☐ **TOOLS**
Utility knife, metal snips (for expanded metal lath), drill/driver, tape measure, cold chisel, wood chisel if needed for undercutting hole

☐ **SKILLS**
Power-driving screws, cutting drywall, applying joint compound, sanding

☐ **MATERIALS**
Expanded metal lath or drywall to match thickness of plaster, setting-type joint compound, regular joint compound, 1-inch drywall screws if lath is intact

Fixing holes

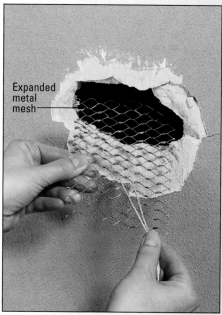

Expanded metal mesh

1 You'll need to replace missing or damaged lath. Cut the plaster with a cold chisel so the hole flares out. Cut a piece of expanded metal mesh that is larger than the hole. Hold it in place with string attached to a bridge made of a piece of 1×2 suspended over two pieces of 2×4.

2 Wet the surrounding plaster, then apply a ¼-inch coat of setting-type joint compound to the mesh. Build up additional coats until the patch is almost flush with the wall surface. Clip the string and apply a final coat of regular joint compound. Sand the patch smooth.

Repairing sagging plaster

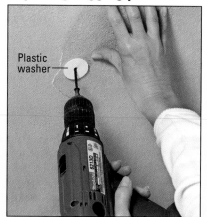

Plastic washer

You may be able to stabilize loose plaster by screwing it to the underlying lath. Use plastic plaster washers, available at professional drywall suppliers.

WHAT IF...
An entire wall needs to be replaced?

Sometimes in an older house you may be faced with a plaster wall that is beyond repair. It may be too rough, have too many cracks, or have extensive water damage. In this case you have two choices: Tear out the whole mess, which is no small job between the demolition and the cleanup, or cover the wall with a new layer of drywall.

If you choose to cover, use ¼-inch drywall. Spread drywall mastic on the back of the sheets. Try to locate the studs in the wall and screw the drywall to them. Use 2½-inch drywall screws to penetrate the drywall, the plaster, and the studs. Finish the drywall as you would any drywall-covered wall.

Fixing larger areas

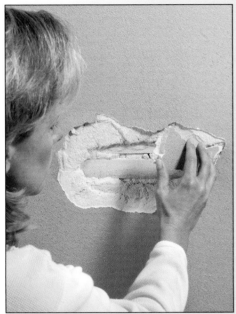

1 For a larger repair, remove all of the damaged plaster, including pieces that feel loose. Cut a piece of drywall that is approximately the same size as the damaged area. Use drywall that is as close as possible to but not thicker than the thickness of the plaster.

2 Screw the drywall in place. Work carefully so the screws don't strip out in the lath. Don't use nails—the pounding causes further damage.

3 Build up the patch with a layer of setting-type joint compound until it is almost flush with the surface. Do this in two coats if the plaster is more than ¼ inch thicker than the drywall. Tape the seams with mesh tape, then finish the job with regular joint compound.

Repairing cracks in plaster

Hairline cracks are tough to fix, because it is difficult to get more than a little filler into them. Wet the crack and surrounding wall with a squirt bottle first, then press ready-mixed joint compound as firmly as possible into the crack. When it dries, sand smooth.

For cracks wider than ¼ inch, undercut the edges to help the patch stay in place. Chip away at the plaster with a wood chisel (doing so dulls a chisel, so use one you don't plan on using for woodworking). Brush away all debris.

Tape helps: After undercutting, wet the crack, pack it with setting-type joint compound, and smooth the compound even with the surface. After the first coat dries, tape over the crack with mesh tape and coat with regular joint compound. Feather the edges widely to blend with the wall.

INSTALLING A DROPPED CEILING

A dropped ceiling (also called a suspended ceiling) consists of a metal grid and the acoustical tiles it supports. The grid is hung from framing or an existing ceiling. It consists of wall molding around the perimeter; main runners, which run across the width of the ceiling; and cross tees, which go between the main runners. Depending on the tiles used, main runners are spaced 24 or 48 inches on center. The cross tees are also placed to fit the tiles.

Dropped ceilings require no taping or mudding, so installing one generates no dust. As a result, a dropped ceiling is a comparatively convenient fix for a deteriorated plaster ceiling. Dropped ceilings allow access to the space above, which works well in a basement where plumbing valves or electrical junction boxes are located. The space above them makes a handy wiring chase for running low-voltage wires (for telephones, TVs, or stereo speakers) with a minimum of fuss.

PRESTART CHECKLIST

☐ **TIME**
About 6 to 8 hours for a 10×10-foot room

☐ **TOOLS**
Tape measure, chalk line, line level, clamps, 4-foot level, drill/driver, metal snips, utility knife

☐ **SKILLS**
Measuring and laying out, snapping chalk lines, driving screws, cutting thin gauge metal, cutting acoustical panels

☐ **PREP**
Walls should be as complete as possible, including paint

☐ **MATERIALS**
Wall molding, main runners, cross tees, hanging wire, screws, hanger screws, acoustical panels

1 Measure the room and draw a floor plan. Then measure the ceiling height. Most grid systems require at least 3 inches of free space above. Place the grid low enough to clear pipes or anything else hanging down, but high enough to clear window and door tops.

Line level

2 Slip a line level onto your chalk line and make adjustments. Snap a level line around the perimeter of the room, indicating the top of the wall molding. Double-check the line with a 4-foot level.

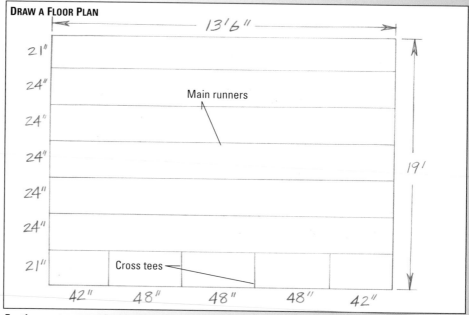

DRAW A FLOOR PLAN

13'6"

21"
24"
24"
24"
24"
24"
21"

Main runners

Cross tees

19'

42"   48"   48"   48"   42"

For the most symmetrical look, start your layout in the center of each side and work your way toward the edges. If necessary, adjust the layout so spaces at the perimeter are at least half a panel wide.

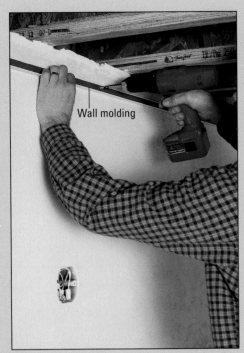

3 Screw the wall molding to the studs with its top edge even with the snapped lines. Butt the pieces together to make longer runs.

4 Mark the main runner locations on the wall molding. Stretch a string along their path to indicate the level of the bottom of the runners.

5 Suspend main runners within 2 feet of the end walls and every 4 feet between. Turn hanger screws into the joists or ceiling above the runners. Hang wires from the hanger screws. Cut the runner length so holes align under wires. Twist the wires until the top of the runner aligns with the strings.

6 The cross tees are clipped into slots in the main runners. Install them according to the spacing required by the ceiling panels. At the walls, cut the cross tees so their ends rest on the wall molding.

7 When the grid is complete, drop the panels into place. If you need to make some odd-size pieces, cut the panels with a utility knife guided by a straightedge.

STANLEY PRO TIP

Use a laser level for big jobs

If you are installing a drop ceiling in a large room, rent a rotary laser level to establish an initial level line around the perimeter of the room.

Be careful not to look directly into the laser while you are working. Don't leave the laser running while you install the wall molding. Instead snap chalk lines along the laser's path. A laser level is also helpful when installing trim molding, such as a picture frame rail, chair rail, or wainscoting *(pages 113–115)*.

HANGING DOORS

After drywall is hung and finished (and perhaps painted), it's time to hang the doors in their openings. This is when you find out just how good a job you did framing. Walls and openings that are not plumb and square make the job of hanging doors a challenge.

In days gone by, hanging doors was painstaking work, left to one of the top carpenters on a job. The jamb (door frame) had to be joined and assembled, the pieces and the door mortised for the hinges, and the whole thing had to be fitted to the opening. These days, with prehung doors, the task isn't nearly as tricky. It still requires some precision and skill, but it is easily within the reach of most do-it-yourselfers.

Many interior remodeling jobs involve the addition of a closet. For closets, bypass doors and bifold doors are convenient, space-saving alternatives to regular swinging doors. They are also easy to install since they simply hang from tracks and don't need to fit as precisely as a swinging door.

Door construction

Today most doors are constructed in one of three ways. The least expensive are called "hollow-core," so named because their inside structure consists of corrugated cardboard. Their exteriors can be flush (flat) plywood or hardboard that's molded to look like raised panel doors.

In the midprice range are "solid-core" doors, which have a wood fiber core covered with a veneer of wood or paintable hardboard. You'll pay a premium for solid wood doors. These have wooden rails (crosspieces) and stiles (vertical pieces) that surround solid wood panels.

Reusing doors

The job does become more complicated when you want to reuse doors that are not prehung. They may have been salvaged from the remodeling job, or they could be used doors that you have acquired from another source. But why bother to reuse a door? For the same reasons it is worth recycling almost anything: You'll save money over buying new doors, particularly if you want solid-wood, raised-panel construction, and you may be able to match details to other doors and trim in your house.

Prehung doors take the difficulty out of installing doors.

CHAPTER PREVIEW

Installing a prehung door
page 88

Installing bypass doors
page 92

Installing bifold doors
page 93

Hanging an old door in new jambs
page 94

Check your work often as you install doors. Keeping the jamb plumb is especially important.

Precut wood shims are a must for hanging doors. They are sold in packages at home centers and hardware stores.

Take your time when hanging doors. Not only does careful craftsmanship look good, you will benefit from it every time you open or close the door.

Fitting a new door to an existing opening
page 96

Tuning up an old door
page 98

INSTALLING A PREHUNG DOOR

Working with a prehung unit takes a lot of the demanding precision work out of installing a door. Hinge mortises and holes for the lockset and strike are already cut. But you still need to work carefully for best results. One of the most important things you can do to make installing doors easier is to make sure your framing is well-made. A rough opening that is plumb and square is far easier to deal with than one that isn't. Keep double-checking as you build and take the time to fix mistakes as they occur, rather than hoping they will be hidden by the next step.

If you are hanging a door in an older house, keep an eye on the big picture. Before setting the nails, step back and look at your work. Even if you have plumbed the door, if the wall or floor is off level or plumb, you may want to align the door frame at least a little bit with its surroundings to make sure it looks right. For example, if the wall leans slightly, match the jamb to the wall. It won't be noticeable as long as the door doesn't lean enough to open and close by itself.

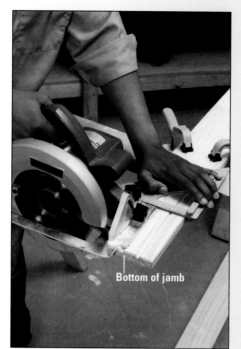

Bottom of jamb

1 Tap out the hinge pins with a screwdriver and hammer. Remove the door. Slip the frame into the doorway and check the head jamb for level. If it isn't, shim under the jamb on the low side. Measure the shimmed space; then remove this amount from the opposite jamb.

2 Check that the jack stud on the hinge side of the opening is plumb. Also check to see if the wall leans one way or the other. If the jack stud is plumb, nail the jamb directly to it with 16d finish nails, two below each hinge and two near the center.

PRESTART CHECKLIST

☐ **TIME**
About 2 hours per door

☐ **TOOLS**
4-foot level, circular saw, layout square, hammer, nail set, utility knife

☐ **SKILLS**
Crosscutting, driving nails, checking for plumb

☐ **PREP**
Doorway should be framed and drywall applied to both sides

☐ **MATERIALS**
Prehung door, shims, 16d finishing nails, 8d finish nails

WHAT IF ...
You are planning to install hardwood flooring or tile?

The typical prehung door comes with a 1¼-inch gap at the bottom of the door. This allows for clearance above a carpet and its pad (about 1 inch). If you plan to install hardwood floors, which are ¾ inch thick, you'll need to cut down the jambs by ⅞ inch (¾ inch for the floor plus ⅛ inch to reduce the gap under the door). This allows the flooring to run under the ends of the jambs. If the floor under the doorway isn't level, you'll need to adjust the jambs as shown in Step 1 above. Tile thicknesses vary as does the thickness of the mastic bed, so check these in advance. Allow ¼ inch between tile and door bottom.

After cutting the jambs to the right length to accommodate hardwood flooring, use spacer blocks to position the jambs in the doorway. Make the spacers from scraps of your finish floor material.

3 If the hinge-side stud is not plumb, nail either the top or bottom, whichever is closer to the center of the opening. Insert shims at the opposite end to make the jamb plumb. Below the shims, drive two 16d finish nails just far enough to hold the shims and jambs in place. Adjust shims if necessary.

4 Before setting nails, check that the hinge jamb is centered across the wall thickness. A typical jamb is slightly wider than the wall thickness to allow for irregularities in the drywall. If adjustment is necessary, pull the nails, protecting the jamb with a scrap under the hammer.

5 Put the door back on its hinges and swing it closed. Insert shims between the jamb and the stud about halfway between the hinges and adjust them until the gap between the door and jamb is equal from top to bottom. Open the door and drive two 16d finish nails below the shims.

Dealing with doors: Which hand is which?

If you have to order the doors you want, you may end up in a discussion over whether you want a right- or a left-handed door. This can be confusing, in part because locksets and doors use the same terminology but in slightly different ways.

For doors: If the hinges are on the left and you have to pull the door open, it is a left-handed door, as shown at left. If the hinges are on the right when you pull the door, it's a right-handed door.

For locksets, the "hand" is determined from outside the room. If the door swings into the room and the hinges are on the left, the lockset is left-hand, as shown at right. If the door swings out of the room and the hinges are on the left, the lockset is left-hand reverse. If hinges are on the right, the door can be right-hand or right-hand reverse.

The best way to avoid confusion is to to draw diagrams of exactly what you want; then show the diagrams to your supplier.

STANLEY PRO TIP

Check for hidden bumps

When prehung doors are assembled, the hinge screws sometimes poke through the back of the jamb, and these little nubs are enough to throw a jamb out of plumb. File them flat before installing the door frame.

Installing a prehung door (continued)

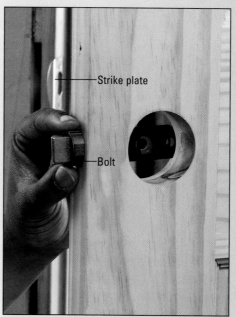

Strike plate

Bolt

A playing card provides the right amount of space between a prefinished door and stop.

6 The strike side of the frame is also nailed in three places: top, bottom, and middle. Insert shims and adjust so the gap between the door and the jamb is even, top to bottom. Nail the jamb in place with pairs of 16d nails driven just below the shims.

7 To get the doorstops placed properly, screw the strike plate to the jamb, slip the bolt into the door, and screw it in place. There is no need to install the entire lockset at this time.

8 On many prehung units, the doorstops are only temporarily attached, to be mounted permanently after the unit is in place. Pry the stops free. Close the door and hold it tightly against the strike plate. Nail the stops in place while holding them against the door.

WHAT IF ...
The jack stud is twisted?

One common problem you may come up against when installing a prehung door is a twisted jack stud. Even if you carefully select framing lumber and craft the wall frame accurately, it is possible for the studs to move as they adjust to conditions in the house. The result is often a door opening that isn't true. If you attach a door frame to a twisted jack stud, it will look as though the door is standing partially open; actually the entire doorframe will be protruding into the room.

You can force the frame back into the plane of the wall, but doing so runs the risk of damaging the frame. Adding a third shim to each pair of shims that locates the jamb returns the frame to its position without adding stress to the door frame assembly.

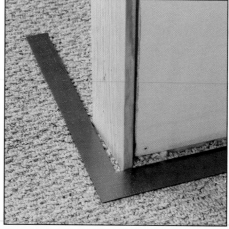

A twisted jack stud won't allow a door frame to stand properly in its opening.

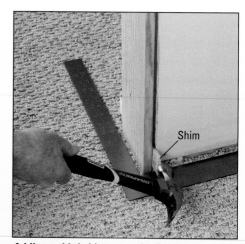

Shim

Adding a third shim to a pair of shims compensates for the twisted jack stud and allows the door frame to assume a proper square position.

9 If the door and jamb are to be painted, use a matchbook cover as a spacer between the door and stop as you nail the stop in place. This allows for the thickness of the paint on the various surfaces.

10 When you are satisfied with the fit of the door within the frame, and the frame within the opening, drive 8d finish nails through the jambs and shims to lock the shims in place. Cut off the shims with a utility knife or handsaw.

11 As a final step, replace two of the screws in each hinge with longer screws that reach into the jack studs. The door hangs from the jack studs, not just from the jambs.

STANLEY PRO TIP: **There's more than one way to plumb a door**

To install door frames efficiently, you need a long level. A 48-inch model is adequate, but a 72-inch level is the best tool to use. If you don't want to invest in either of these tools, there is another approach. Instead of a level, you can use a plumb bob to check whether the jambs are plumb or not. To use this method, secure the hinge-side jamb to the jack stud with three pairs of shims as shown on *page 89*. Drive a 16d finish nail partially into the jamb near the top (the stop will eventually cover the hole). Hang a plumb bob from the nail so it dangles almost to the floor. Adjust the shims until the gap between the jamb and the string is equal from top to bottom. Pin the shims in place with 8d finish nails.

Hang a plumb bob alongside a door jamb to give yourself an immediate reference for plumbing the jamb. This simple tool eliminates the need for a long level when installing doors.

Adjust the shims behind the jamb until the distance from the jamb to the string is equal all along the length of the jamb. Add pairs of shims if necessary to compensate for a warped jamb.

INSTALLING BYPASS DOORS

The most popular choice for closets, bypass doors need no room to swing open, a plus. But they allow access to only one side of a closet at a time, a minus. Hardware kits are available for openings of 4, 5, 6, and 8 feet. To accommodate other size openings, simply cut the standard tracks with a hacksaw.

The kits are designed to work with standard, 1⅜-inch-thick interior doors. If you use thicker doors, they may interfere with each other as they open and close. Thinner doors may have a wide gap between them. The combined width of the doors should equal the width of the opening plus at least 1 inch. This provides ½ inch of overlap between the two doors.

Some minor variations exist between bypass door kits from different manufacturers, but they are all easy to install. Just be sure to check the manufacturer's directions carefully before you start.

PRESTART CHECKLIST

☐ **TIME**
About 1 hour for a pair of doors

☐ **TOOLS**
Drill/driver, level, tape measure

☐ **SKILLS**
Leveling the track, locating and installing hardware

☐ **PREP**
Finish the opening with wood jambs or drywall; casings can be installed later

☐ **MATERIALS**
Bypass door hardware kit, doors, shims

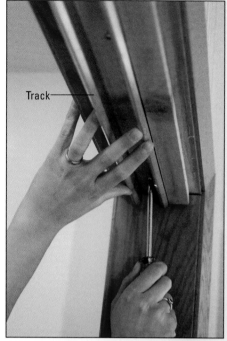

1 The location of the track depends on how you plan to trim the opening. Consult the manufacturer's instructions. Screw the track to the top of the door opening. Check to make sure the track is level; shim if necessary.

2 Attach the hangers to the tops of the doors. The hardware kit specifies exact locations. Tip the doors to hook the hangers onto the track. After the doors are hanging, install the center guide on the floor to keep the doors in line.

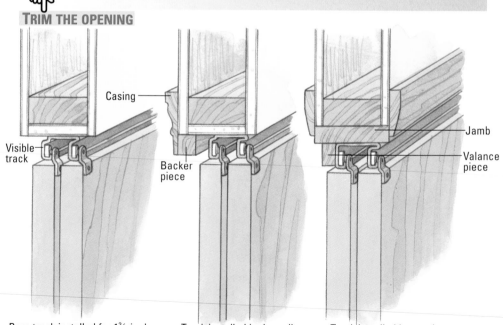

TRIM THE OPENING

Bare track installed for 1⅜-inch doors in drywall opening

Track installed in drywall opening hidden with casing.

Track installed in opening with regular jamb and casing

When hanging bypass doors, you have some options for finishing the opening. For utility applications, simply hang the doors as is (left). For a more finished look, add trim to the header (middle and right).

INSTALLING BIFOLD DOORS

Bifold doors can be installed easily in almost any opening in your home. They can be used for closet doors, for privacy, or for controlling heat and airflow between rooms. Their chief advantages include ease of installation and a minimum of swing space required. However, they take up more space in the door opening than do swinging doors.

Commonly available with plastic, metal, or wooden doors, bifold door kits come in a variety of styles, including louvered, paneled, and smooth. The kits fit most standard-width openings, although the maximum width of a single door is 24 inches. Units can be combined to cover openings up to 16 feet wide. Wooden doors can be trimmed for a better fit; plastic doors cannot be trimmed. (Keep in mind, if you trim a wooden door kit, each door must be trimmed equally.) Two heights are available—one to fit standard 6-foot 8-inch openings, the other for 8-foot floor-to-ceiling applications.

PRESTART CHECKLIST

☐ **TIME**
About 1 hour for a pair of doors

☐ **TOOLS**
Drill/driver, level, tape measure

☐ **SKILLS**
Leveling the track, locating and installing hardware

☐ **PREP**
The opening should be complete with wooden jambs or drywall hung and finished; casings can be installed later

☐ **MATERIALS**
Bifold door hardware kit, doors, shims

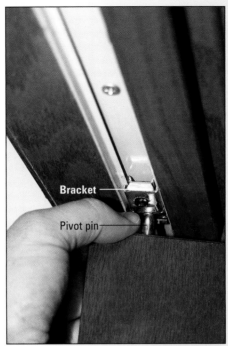

Bracket

Pivot pin

1 Bifold doors require a track similar to that used by bypass doors. Screw the track to the top of the opening. The doors pivot on pins protruding from their top and bottom. These pins engage brackets attached to the floor or jamb and the track.

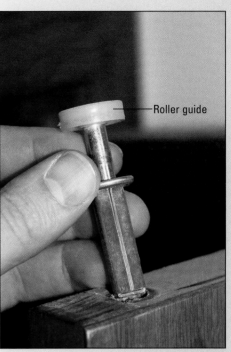

Roller guide

2 Attach the roller or pin guide to the free end of the doors. This guide rides in the track and keeps the door in alignment.

BIFOLD DOOR TRIM OPTIONS

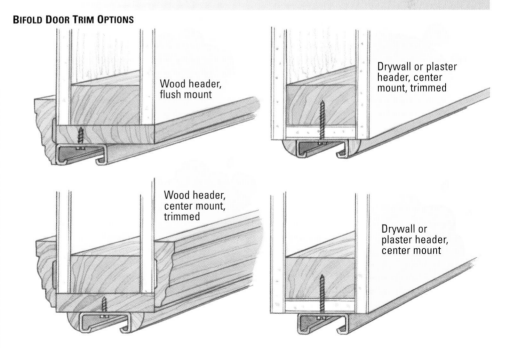

Wood header, flush mount

Drywall or plaster header, center mount, trimmed

Wood header, center mount, trimmed

Drywall or plaster header, center mount

As with bypass doors, you have trim options when installing a bifold door, depending on the look you are after.

HANGING AN OLD DOOR IN NEW JAMBS

If you wish to reuse an old door, purchase a door frame, sometimes called a "jamb kit" at a lumberyard or home center. The kit consists of three pieces of $\frac{9}{16}$-inch-thick lumber that's $4\frac{5}{8}$ inches wide. The two side jambs have a groove, called a dado, or a ledge, called a rabbet, across the top to receive the third piece, which is called the head jamb.

The first step is to make the door fit the opening, or vice versa. A properly sized door is about $2\frac{1}{4}$ inches narrower than the rough opening and 1 inch shorter than the distance from the header to the finished floor. If you have to cut a door a significant amount in width, trim from both edges to keep the stiles symmetrical. With hollow-core doors, try not to cut beyond the solid edges. If you have to cut into the hollow area, save the solid edges and glue them back into the door to reinforce it.

PRESTART CHECKLIST

☐ **TIME**
About 1 to 3 hours

☐ **TOOLS**
Tape measure, table saw, circular saw, layout square, router, chisels, drill/driver

☐ **SKILLS**
Measuring and laying out, ripping on a table saw, crosscutting with a circular saw, routing hinge mortises, trimming with a chisel, driving screws

☐ **PREP**
Door opening should be framed, used door should be square and flat

☐ **MATERIALS**
Jamb kit, $2\frac{1}{2}$-inch screws, doorstop molding

Head jamb rabbet

1 If the floor will be carpeted, hook the tape measure into the side jamb rabbets or dadoes and measure down a distance that is $1\frac{5}{16}$ inch more than the length of the door. Cut the jambs to this length. If you will be adding a finished wood floor, remove an extra $\frac{7}{8}$ inch (page 88).

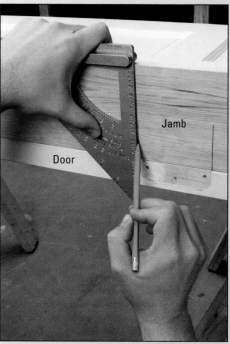
Jamb
Door

2 Hold the hinge jamb along the edge of the door and lay out the hinge locations on the jamb. The top of the door should be just slightly more than $\frac{1}{16}$ inch below the edge of the rabbet or dado. Mark the mortise locations with a sharp pencil.

WHAT IF ...
The door needs new hinge mortises?

With many previously used doors, you may want to trim the edge of the door to eliminate the old hinge mortises. This gives you a chance to start fresh with the placement of the hinges. It also means you don't have to try to find hinges that match the old mortises.

Locating the new hinges doesn't have to be especially precise as long as the mortises on the door match those on the jamb. Most doors require three hinges (hollow-core doors only need two). Center the middle hinge and locate the top and bottom hinges about 6 inches from the ends of the door.

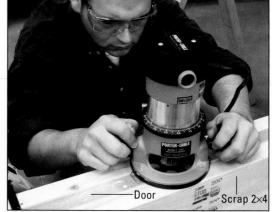
Door
Scrap 2×4

Cut the mortises in the door first. Clamp some 2×4 scraps on either side of the door to keep the router from tipping. Square the mortise with a chisel, then transfer the locations to the jamb.

3 Use a utility knife to scribe the hinge leaf outline onto the door edge. Set a ½-inch straight router bit slightly deeper than the hinge leaf thickness. Rout close to the scribe lines. Tune the mortise with a chisel.

4 Cut the head jamb to a length equal to the door width plus the combined rabbet or dado depth plus slightly more than ⅛ inch. Screw the door frame together with 2½-inch screws. Attach the hinges to the jamb and the door.

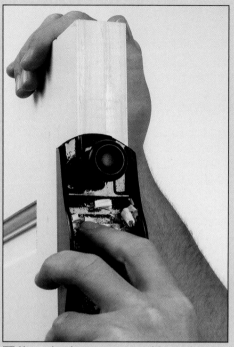

5 Hang the door as you would a prehung unit. Check its fit in the opening before securing the jamb. Plane the strike-side edge of the door if necessary. Cut the doorstop and install it as shown on *pages 90–91*.

WHAT IF …
You don't have a router?

Edge of jamb

1 You can cut hinge mortises by hand with a chisel. Hold the hinge in place and scribe around it with a utility knife. Mark the depth of the mortise on the edge of the jamb with your knife, using a combination square as a guide. The depth of the mortise must be slightly more than the thickness of the hinge leaf.

2 Sharpen your widest chisel (1 inch to 1½ inches is best). Cut down close to the mortise depth all around the perimeter of the mortise.

3 Once you have defined the outline of the mortise, pare away the rest of the material until the mortise is cut to its full depth. Try to keep the bottom of the mortise as flat as possible so the hinge sits flat.

FITTING A NEW DOOR TO AN EXISTING OPENING

No rule says you have to match your new door and trim to what is already in the room. If your existing doors lack style, or if it is simply time for a change, you can refit existing doorways with new doors. If you are lucky, you will be able to reuse the hinges and other hardware.

Think twice before deciding to replace the trim, a much bigger job. Swapping doors makes a big visual difference, without requiring a lot of labor. Replacing trim makes a more subtle visual difference and requires more time and effort.

Unless your house is very old, you'll have little problem finding doors to fit. The most common door height is 80 inches, although most models are available 78 inches tall as well. Commonly available interior door widths are 24, 28, 30, 32, and 36 inches.

PRESTART CHECKLIST

☐ **TIME**
About 1½ to 2 hours to hang a new door

☐ **TOOLS**
Tape measure, block plane, square, router, chisels, drill/driver, 2⅛-inch hole saw, 1-inch spade bit

☐ **SKILLS**
Measuring and laying out, planing, cutting mortises, drilling

☐ **PREP**
Remove old door, acquire new hardware if necessary

☐ **MATERIALS**
New door, new hardware (if needed), shims, matchbooks

1 Measure the opening and purchase a door that fits. If you have to trim the door, take an equal amount off each side. Plane a slight bevel (approximately 5 degrees) on the strike side of the door to ease opening and closing.

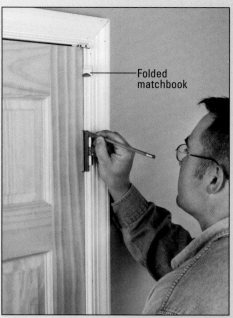

Folded matchbook

2 Check the door's fit. Ideally there should be a gap of slightly more than ¹⁄₁₆ inch at the top and along each side, and about ⅜ inch at the bottom. Use spacers made from folded matchbooks (four thicknesses equals about ¹⁄₁₆ inch) along with shims underneath to maintain the spacing. Mark the mortise locations and cut the mortises as described on *pages 94–95*.

STANLEY PRO TIP: **Mortising jigs**

If you have more than one or two doors to hang, consider investing in a hinge-mortising jig. These templates guide a router to cut perfect mortises for hinges. Several models are on the market. The simplest (and least expensive) models cut one mortise at a time, leaving the placement of the matching mortise up to you. The more complex jigs come with several templates and will position the mortises on both the jamb and the edge of the door.

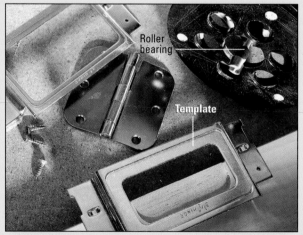

Roller bearing

Template

Most hinge-mortising jigs work with a router equipped with a template guide. The guide could be a roller bearing on the bit, as shown here, or a metal collar attached to the router's base that surrounds the bit and runs along the mortise template.

3 Hang the door. New locksets come with a template to help you locate where to drill holes. If you are reusing a lockset, extend a line across the face of the door with your square, making sure it is centered on the strike plate. Measure the lockset to determine the distance the hole should be from the edge of the door. Drill a 2⅛-inch hole through the door with a hole saw.

4 For the bolt, drill a 1-inch hole through the edge of the door for the bolt with a spade bit. Make sure the hole is centered from front to back and aligned with the center of the strike plate.

5 Insert the bolt into the hole in the door's edge. Align the bolt plate with the edges of the door and trace around it with your utility knife. Remove the bolt and cut away the wood inside the outline to create a mortise for the plate. When finished, the plate should lie slightly below the surface.

WHAT IF ...
There are no hinge mortises in the opening?

Some houses have openings that have been trimmed out like a doorway with jambs and casings, but no door. These might be found, for example, between a kitchen and dining room or between a den and a hallway. If you decide to add a door, you'll need to cut mortises in the jambs to hang the door and to install doorstops.

If you're dealing with an opening that is finished only with drywall, you may be able to treat it similarly to a rough opening and install a prehung door. If the rough opening was framed to a standard size and ½-inch drywall was used, check to see if the opening is square. If it is, you can nail the door frame directly against the drywall opening. Otherwise you'll need to remove the corner bead and the drywall from the jamb and header faces to make room for shims.

1 Check carefully for nails, then lay out the hinge mortises on the jamb. Rout close to the layout lines. Finish the mortises with a sharp chisel. Hold the door in the opening with shims and transfer the marks

2 After the door is hung and the lockset installed, rub a little lipstick on the bolt to mark the jamb for the strike plate. Using a spade bit, drill a 1-inch hole for the bolt; mortise the strike plate into the jamb with a chisel.

TUNING UP AN OLD DOOR

As a house ages, its various parts often shift out of their original positions. This inevitable settling can add a bit of charm to a structure, but it can also cause problems. This is especially true of doors, which are particularly sensitive to subtle shifts in their frames. Since you're in a remodeling mood, you may as well tune up any doors that aren't behaving the way they should.

Depending on the age of your house, this tune-up could be as simple as tightening a few screws, or it could mean planing down a few high spots before applying a new coat of paint.

If you live in a cold climate and need to plane a sticky door, it is a good idea to wait until the most humid part of the summer to do it. Doors swell up when it is humid, so if you plane just enough to allow the door to close in the summer, you know it will work when it shrinks in the dry winter weather.

Note: If you plane the edge of a door, paint or apply finish to that edge as soon as possible to hinder moisture absorption.

Tighten the screws: To fix a loose or sticking door, first tighten the hinge screws. Over time, screws slowly work loose, causing a door to sag slightly in its opening.

Use longer screws: If the screws won't tighten but simply turn in their holes, the holes are stripped. Remove the old screws and replace them with longer ones.

PRESTART CHECKLIST

☐ **TIME**
15 to 30 minutes per door

☐ **TOOLS**
Screwdriver, block plane, utility knife, straightedge, circular saw

☐ **SKILLS**
Driving screws, planing, cutting with a circular saw

☐ **MATERIALS**
2½-inch screws, dry lubricant

STANLEY PRO TIP: **Use steel for strength, brass for good looks**

Carpenters often install doors with brass hardware and brass hinges. Brass is a nice material for hardware because it looks nice, even as it ages. Unfortunately brass screws are not very strong. They hold well enough, but they are tricky to drive in without damaging the slots or twisting the heads right off. To get around these problems, purchase a few steel screws that are the same size as the brass ones you are using. Drive the steel screws in first to cut the threads in the wood. Then replace the steel screws with the brass ones.

No matter what kind of screws you are driving, they will go in easier if you lubricate them with a little wax. Don't use soap—it attracts moisture, which causes corrosion.

Plane to fit: If the door still sticks, check the edge to see where it is rubbing. Often wear marks indicate where the door is contacting the jamb. Plane down the high spots with a block plane.

Adding clearance: If the door rubs the floor (or carpet), it needs to be cut. Remove the door and place it on a pair of sawhorses padded with towels or carpet scraps. Using a metal straightedge and a utility knife, deeply scribe a cut line across the door to reduce splintering. Cut with a circular saw.

A touch of lubricant: As you rehang the door, squirt a little dry lubricant, such as graphite, in the hinges and on the hinge pins. Doing so eliminates squeaks and groans from the hinges.

Cutting a hollow-core door

Hollow core

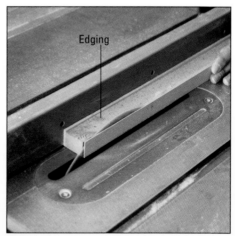

Edging

1 Hollow-core doors are reinforced with solid edges for attaching hardware and to allow slight trimming. If you cut one down past this edge, you will expose the door's hollow core. This doesn't make the door unusable.

2 If you need to cut down a hollow-core door significantly (past the edging), save the edging that you cut off. On a table saw, cut the facings off the edging to make it the right thickness to be reinserted in the door.

3 Glue and clamp the edging between the two door faces. When the glue dries, the door will be ready to go.

INSTALLING MOLDINGS

Trim—the moldings around doors, windows, walls, and ceilings—serves two purposes. The first is practical: It covers and disguises seams, gaps, and rough edges. In this role it creates a transition between different materials and eases discrepancies where one surface doesn't quite align with another. The second purpose is aesthetic: Trim does much to determine the style of a room, be it colonial, Victorian, contemporary, or something else.

Molding terms
In this chapter you'll learn how to apply casing around door and window frames, baseboard where a wall meets the floor, and crown molding at the junction of walls and ceiling. You'll also learn how to install chair rail, a protective molding placed about halfway up a wall, and picture molding, a piece attached about 18 inches down from the ceiling. And you'll find instructions for installing wainscoting, a decorative paneling that covers the bottom half of a wall.

Types of moldings
In the days before the Industrial Revolution, moldings were handcrafted specifically for the places they were to be installed. When mass-production reached the lumber and millwork industry, moldings became more standardized. Currently a trade group—the Wood Moulding and Millwork Producers Association—has established a series of standard molding profiles that are identified by numbers in a pattern book. These profiles are probably available at your local home center or lumberyard. While all the profiles may not be in stock, you should be able to order exactly what you need. If you are looking for something different, a woodworking shop can create the design you want, but be warned: Custom moldings are not cheap. You also can mill your own moldings, if you are willing to invest in the proper cutters and setups for your router.

Practice for perfection
Careful work is important in every aspect of a remodeling project, but the trim, which is on display every day in your new room, advertises the pride you take in your work. Take time to practice the techniques used to connect molding pieces before you tackle the most visible areas of your project. Don't be afraid to reject a piece of molding that doesn't fit just right. You'll probably be able to use it elsewhere.

Trim serves practical and decorative purposes, and puts your finish carpentry skills on display.

CHAPTER PREVIEW

Cutting miter joints
page 102

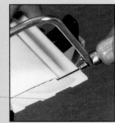

Cutting coped joints
page 104

Installing door and window casing
page 106

Installing baseboard
page 108

The trim elements you choose define the architectural character of your home.

Installing crown molding
page 110

Installing chair rail and picture frame molding
page 113

Installing wainscoting
page 114

STANLEY PRO TIP

Predrilling prevents nailing problems

When installing hardwood molding, predrill holes for all finishing nails to help prevent them from bending. Predrilling is also a good idea for softwood molding; doing so prevents splitting whenever you are nailing within about 6 inches of the end of a piece. If you don't have a bit of the right diameter, clip off the head of one of the finishing nails and chuck it into your drill. Another way to prevent splitting near the end of a board is to blunt the nail tips with a couple of hammer taps before you drive them in.

CUTTING MITER JOINTS

The miter joint, where the ends of the pieces to be joined are cut at an angle (usually 45 degrees), is one of three joints used most often to install trim. The others are the coped joint *(pages 104–105)* and the butt joint *(page 106).* Miter joints are used for outside corners, while coped joints handle most of the inside ones. Both allow the molding profiles to continue around a corner without interruption.

To cut miters quickly and accurately, you can use a power miter saw, commonly called a chop saw, or a handsaw and a miter box. Most professionals use a chop saw for its speed and accuracy. A miter box can be just as accurate; however, it takes longer to make a cut by hand. If your budget is tight and you plan to do a limited amount of trim work, opt for a miter box. You can buy a professional-quality integrated miter box and saw for the price of an entry-level chop saw.

Practice making miter cuts on pieces of scrap, both to improve your skills and to check the accuracy of your tools.

1 Set your saw to cut a 45-degree angle with the blade angled to the left. Make a test cut in a scrap piece of molding. Swing the saw to cut a 45-degree angle with the blade angled to the right. Make a matching cut in a second scrap piece held on the other side of the blade.

2 Check to see if a saw makes accurate 45-degree cuts by holding the test pieces together against a framing square. There should be no gap in the joint. If the saw's stops are not set correctly, consult the owner's manual for how to adjust the saw.

Improve the grip of your saw

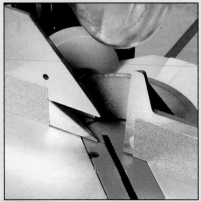

Whether you use a chop saw or a miter box, the workpiece tends to slide when you make an angled cut. To solve this problem, glue a piece of fine sandpaper to the fence with spray adhesive; it will grip the wood.

REFRESHER COURSE
Buying the right blade

Most chop saws come equipped with a coarse saw blade, which is good for cutting 2×4s and other framing lumber but won't do a good job on trim. For making precise miter cuts you'll need a fine crosscutting blade. Such blades have more teeth than general-purpose blades do. Look for a blade that has at least 50–80 teeth ground with an alternate tooth bevel (ATB) pattern. ATB blades excel at crosscutting cleanly; the teeth are ground to shear the wood fibers at the edge of the cut.

If you have a choice, a smaller-diameter blade with more teeth makes much finer cuts than its larger cousin. The smaller diameter means the blade won't wobble as much. The trade-off is that the smaller blade won't cut as wide a piece, but that's not usually an issue when installing trim.

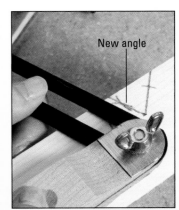

3 Place the test pieces in position. If the miter is open on the outside, adjust the saw to slightly less than 45 degrees. Make test cuts until the angle mates perfectly with one of the original test pieces. Cut one of the pieces you'll install to the adjusted angle, the other to exactly 45 degrees.

4 If the test pieces are open at the back when you place them against the wall, you need to set the saw at slightly more than 45 degrees. Cut scrap until you find the right angle, then cut the angle on one piece you'll install and an exact 45-degree angle on the other installation piece.

5 If you have to make very subtle changes to the miter angle, you may find it easier to insert shims behind the molding rather than trying to shift the blade a slight amount. Plastic-coated playing cards work well for this job; keep a deck in your toolbox.

WHAT IF ...
The corner isn't 90 degrees?

With corners that are slightly off 90 degrees, you can achieve a close fit for miter joints by cutting one molding piece to exactly 45 degrees and then making minor adjustments to the saw to "sneak up" on the matching angle for the other piece.

For corners that are intentionally far from square, you'll have to reset the saw to split the angle in half. Fortunately this is easy to do without math calculations. You just need a T-bevel and a compass.

1 Set a T-bevel against the corner to set the angle. Transfer the angle you want to a board.

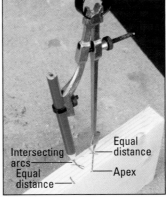

Intersecting arcs — Equal distance
Equal distance — Apex

2 Starting at the apex, mark an equal distance along each leg of the angle with a compass. From these new points, draw two intersecting arcs with the same compass setting.

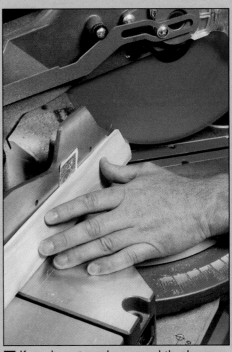

New angle

3 Draw a line through the apex of the angle and the point where the arcs intersect. This line bisects the original angle. Transfer the new angle to the saw via the T-bevel.

CUTTING COPED JOINTS

Use coped joints instead of miters for an inside corner. You might have difficulty fitting inside miters because the wall surfaces tend to give slightly as you nail the pieces in place. Thus a miter joint that looks perfect when held up for a test fit is likely to gap when nailed in place. A coped joint, on the other hand, accommodates such variations.

A coped joint is essentially a butt joint in which one piece of molding runs right into the corner. The end of the adjoining piece is cut to match the profile of the first piece and butts up against it. This is not as difficult as it may sound; coped joints are much easier to cut than they look, and they are fairly forgiving of inaccuracies. The principal tool used is a coping saw.

Even the pros don't cut perfect copes every time. The trick is to take your time and leave the moldings a little long to begin with so you can "sneak up" on the perfect fit by fine-tuning the cut.

1 Start a coped joint by butting one of the pieces of molding into the corner and fastening it in place. When deciding which piece to cope, choose the one that will be least visible as you enter a room.

2 To reveal the line you will cope, miter-cut the end of the piece as though you were going to make an inside miter.

Fine tune the fit

A small round file works best for fine-tuning coped joints. Filing is slower than using a utility knife but gives you more control when you have just a bit of wood to remove.

If molding will receive a different paint color or finish than an adjoining surface, create a crisp transition by prepainting or prefinishing the molding. Touch up nail holes and joints when the molding is installed.

SAFETY FIRST
Supporting long pieces

When cutting long pieces of molding with a chop saw or a miter box, make sure the end you are not cutting is supported at the same level as the saw or box table. The most important reason to do this is safety—trying to hold an unwieldy, unsupported piece in place is dangerous. In addition, it's much easier to make an accurate cut if the piece is properly supported.

THE LINE YOU WILL COPE
Making the line clear

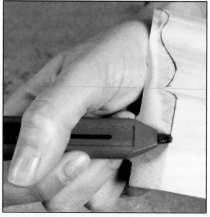

If the molding is prefinished, the profile cut line will show clearly when you make the miter cut. For unfinished molding it can be helpful to run a pencil along the profile to help guide the cut.

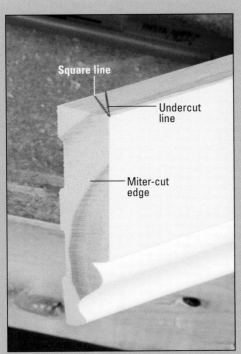

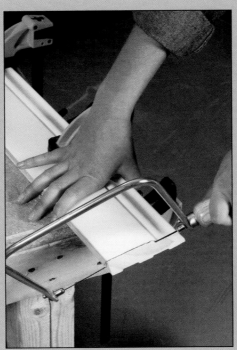

3 In a perfect world, a coped joint would be cut square to the surface (shown by the red line above). In reality, a coped joint is undercut (black line) to accommodate any irregularities in the joint.

4 Saw along the cut line with a coping saw, angling the blade slightly to produce the undercut. Brace the molding on a bench or sawhorse.

5 Check the fit of the cope against the molding in the corner. If necessary, you can trim the piece with a utility knife.

Purchasing molding by the numbers

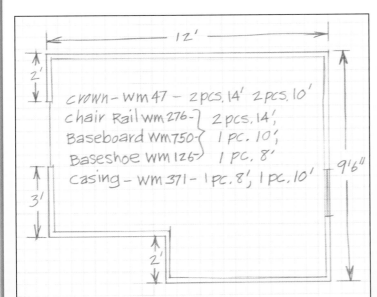

Each standard molding has a number (such as WM 51) assigned by the Wood Moulding and Millwork Producers Association. This number indicates a specific profile and its width. The profiles are illustrated in a pamphlet available from most molding suppliers. When shopping, specify your moldings by the WM number rather than by a name, such as "2¼-inch colonial casing," which might describe several different profiles.

As you calculate how much molding you need, don't simply measure the room and come up with a total number of linear feet. It is better to figure out how long a piece you'll need for each wall and list the moldings that way. This minimizes the number of midwall splices you'll have to make. When listing the lengths needed, add a few extra inches onto each piece to allow for mistakes.

Even when you specify the molding by its WM number, two pieces of the same molding from different suppliers may not match exactly. If possible, select moldings from the same lot number so the profiles match at the joints.

INSTALLING DOOR AND WINDOW CASING

Casing is the word used to describe the molding that frames a door or window opening. In addition to dressing up the opening, casings cover the gaps between the walls and the jambs and hide the raw edge of the drywall. Before wrapping casing around a window or exterior door, loosely fill the gaps with shreds of fiberglass insulation poked in place with a drywall knife or similar tool.

The casings usually are the same throughout a room, if not throughout a house, but that isn't a hard rule. In fact creating a hierarchy of casing details adds visual interest and richness to a room or home. Consider making the casings for exterior doors wider than those for interior doors and windows. Or link the casing size to the size of the opening: Larger openings get larger casings. Use your imagination.

PRESTART CHECKLIST

☐ **TIME**
About 45 minutes to an hour per door

☐ **TOOLS**
Tape measure, chop saw or miter box, hammer, nail set, drill/driver

☐ **SKILLS**
Measuring and laying out, cutting accurate miters, nailing, driving screws

☐ **PREP**
Walls should be finished (and painted, if possible), door should be hung

☐ **MATERIALS**
Molding; 4d, 6d, or 8d finish nails (depending on molding thickness); 2-inch trim head screws

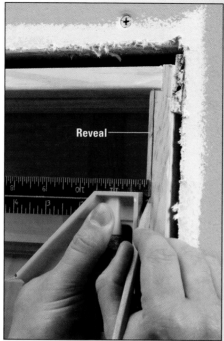

1 Typically casings are positioned to leave ⅛ inch of the jamb's edge visible. This is called the reveal. To lay out the reveal, set a combination square to ⅛ inch, set a pencil in the notch on the edge, and draw a line along the head jamb and both side jambs.

2 Measure from the floor to the head casing reveal on both sides and cut side casings to length. Attach the side casings with five pairs of nails from top to bottom. Allow the nails to protrude in case you have to pull them to trim the casing or adjust its position when you fit the head casing.

TRIM OPTIONS
Cutting butt joints

Miters are necessary if you want a molding profile to continue seamlessly around a door. But if your casings consist of flat boards, it's traditional—and easier—to use butt joints. In a butt joint, the ends of the pieces are cut square and one piece is simply butted up against the other. Most often the head casing sits on top of the side casings, but occasionally the head casing is fitted between the side casings—it's a matter of preference.

During the Victorian era someone invented corner blocks, which added a decorative element while allowing butt joints to be used with ornate molded casings. The blocks are slightly wider and thicker than the casing, making them the most forgiving way to turn the corner around a window or door.

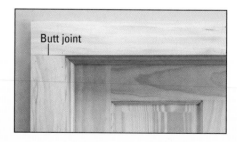

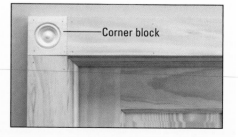

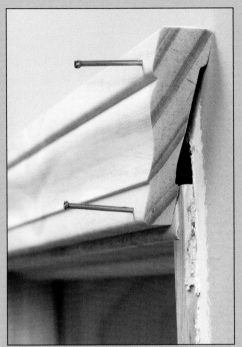

3 Most casings are back cut; that is, they have a shallow channel (or channels) cut in their backs. These channels allow for irregularities in the wall, so the molding can fit tightly against the wall and jamb. When you install casing, drive the nails through the solid edges.

4 Cut the head casing roughly to length. If the molding is mitered as shown here, start with a piece that's long and carefully trim it to fit. For butt-joined head casing, cut one end square and hold it in place to mark for an exact cut on the other side.

5 Nail the head casing to the wall and head jamb with three pairs of nails. As insurance against the miters opening, drill holes in the casing, then drive 2-inch trim head screws through the head casing into the side casings as shown. Set all the nailheads when you are happy with the fit.

Casing a window

Casing a window is just like casing a door, except the casings don't run all the way to the floor. Choose from two options: The traditional style has a sill that protrudes slightly into the room at the bottom of the window. The sill, which is technically called a stool, is the first piece of trim installed. The side casings then butt to the top of the sill. A piece of casing called an apron is applied under the sill as a finishing touch.

In less traditional construction, the sill is eliminated and the casing is wrapped around the window like a picture frame. This technique demands a little more joint-making skill. No clear starting point exists; just pick one of the sides and go from there.

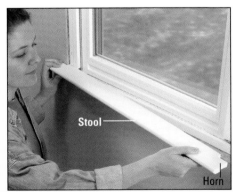

1 Traditional window trim begins with the stool. Use a saber saw to cut the horns on either end so they fit tightly against the drywall and the sides of the jambs.

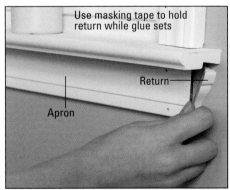

2 The apron is attached under the stool as the final piece of window trim. Measure between the outside of the side casings to determine the apron length. If the apron has a molded profile, miter the ends of the apron toward the wall. Then glue a tiny piece of molding as a return to the wall.

INSTALLING BASEBOARD

Baseboard covers gaps where the floor and the walls come together. It also protects the wall from errant vacuum cleaners, feet, and moving furniture. Aesthetically it eases the transition from vertical to horizontal, adding punctuation to both the wall and floor. Choose baseboard that complements the rest of the trim.

Install baseboard after the walls are painted, the flooring is installed, the door casings are attached, and any built-in cabinetry is in place. If the room is to be carpeted later, use a wider baseboard (¾ inch) so the molding doesn't look too thin after the carpet is in place.

If the baseboard will be painted a different color than the walls, or will meet a finished floor, prime and paint the baseboard before you install it. If you will use base shoe molding, give it two coats of paint before you install it, but don't apply the second paint coat to the baseboard until after you fill the nail holes. This allows you to blend in the shoe while still saving meticulous brush work where moldings meet the wall and the floor.

PRESTART CHECKLIST

☐ **TIME**
About 1½ hours for a room with four walls (including a doorway)

☐ **TOOLS**
Tape measure, chop saw or miter box, hammer, nail set, coping saw, utility knife

☐ **SKILLS**
Measuring and laying out, cutting pieces to length, coping joints, cutting miters

☐ **PREP**
Walls should be finished and painted, door casings in place

☐ **MATERIALS**
Baseboard molding, 8d finishing nails

1 Start installation on the wall opposite the door. Cut baseboard to reach from corner to corner. For runs longer than 5 feet, cut the pieces about ¹⁄₁₆ inch longer than the measurement. The molding will bow slightly so it will press tightly into the corners when nailed in place.

2 Fasten the baseboard with 8d nails driven into the studs and along the bottom plate. Use as many nails as needed to close any gaps between the molding and the wall. Cope the end of the next piece of molding, leaving the other end long for now.

Using multipiece baseboard

While most new houses use a one-piece baseboard, a more traditional approach is to use two or even three pieces of molding to form the baseboard. A multipiece baseboard begins with a piece of baseboard, which is installed first. It is covered with a piece of cap molding, which is small and bends easily to conform to variations in the wall. The final piece is the base shoe. To allow for seasonal movement of a wooden floor, the base shoe is nailed at a slight downward angle into the baseboard, not the floor, with 4d nails. It, too, is quite flexible and disguises gaps between the floor and the underside of the baseboard.

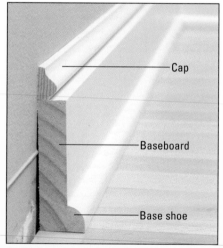

Cap

Baseboard

Base shoe

Multipiece baseboards add a nice touch to the bottom of a wall. Some installations dispense with the cap molding and simply use a baseboard and a shoe molding.

3 After coping the end of the second piece, measure and cut it to length. Again, cut about 1/16 inch long for a tight fit. If the piece runs into a door casing, use a notched piece of plywood to help mark it for length.

4 Outside corners are mitered. Fit the coped end of the molding first, then mark the miter location with the piece in place. Keep in mind that corners are rarely perfectly square. You may need to adjust the miter angles slightly for a good fit. Make test cuts in scrap.

5 If the joint is open at the front, a stroke or two with a block plane at the back of the joint tightens the fit. Another way to change a miter angle slightly is to place a playing card between the chop saw fence and molding, as described on *page 103*.

WHAT IF ...
You have to splice a molding?

It is easier to install moldings that run the full length of a wall, but that isn't always possible. Moldings are available in lengths up to 16 feet (occasionally you can even find 20-footers), but getting these long lengths home can be a problem. And some walls are longer than even the longest pieces available, so you may have to join two pieces.

The best joint to use when splicing is called a scarf joint. You can make a scarf joint by cutting 45-degree angles on the adjoining pieces, which overlap one another. Plan the joint so it falls over a stud for secure nailing. Because the joint occurs at the ends of the pieces, avoid splitting the wood by predrilling the nail holes before driving the nails.

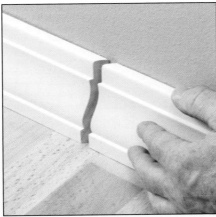

With a little glue and some judicious sanding, a tight-fitting scarf joint practically disappears, especially if the molding is painted after it is installed.

STANLEY PRO TIP

Nail to a solid base

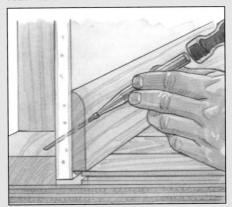

There may be times when you need to drive a nail in a baseboard to eliminate a gap, but a stud isn't where you need it. Drill a hole and drive a 16d finishing nail at a downward angle through the molding to catch the bottom plate.

INSTALLING CROWN MOLDING

Crown molding is installed at the juncture of the wall and the ceiling. Though it looks like a hefty piece of wood, most crown molding is relatively thin material. The secret of its appearance is the way it is installed. Rather than being a solid block nailed into the corner, crown moldings are installed on the diagonal between the wall and ceiling—there is nothing in the corner. Moldings installed this way are said to be "sprung" into place. Because crown moldings are relatively thin, they are flexible enough to conform to irregularities in the wall or ceiling.

The tricky part about installing crown molding is cutting the joints. Because the molding is installed at an angle, it cannot be cut lying flat; as you make the cuts, you must hold it at an angle similar to the way it will be installed.

PRESTART CHECKLIST

☐ **TIME**
About 4 hours for a regular room with four straight walls

☐ **TOOLS**
Tape measure, framing square, miter box or chop saw, hammer, nail set, coping saw, utility knife

☐ **SKILLS**
Measuring and laying out, driving nails, crosscutting moldings, mitering moldings, making coped joints

☐ **PREP**
Walls and ceiling should be finished and painted, molding can be prefinished

☐ **MATERIALS**
Crown molding, 8d finishing nails, wood for blocking

1 Start by determining how far out from the wall the edge of the molding will fall. Hold a piece of the crown inside a framing square to find this measurement. Mark this distance on the ceiling near the corners and at several points along the length of the wall.

2 Start with the wall opposite the door. Cut the molding to length with square cuts on both ends. Hold it in place and nail it first to the wall studs with 8d nails, then to the ceiling joists.

Installing plaster-faced crown molding

In the heyday of the plasterer's craft, elaborate crown moldings in fine homes often were cast in place from plaster rather than made of wood. Today, thanks to a new molding material, you can create the same effect with less skill than it takes to install wood molding. This new material has a very lightweight core of expanded polystyrene—the same material used to make a Styrofoam cup. The polystyrene comes coated with gypsum plaster, so you really are getting a plaster surface.

The good news for do-it-yourselfers is that the molding is attached to the wall with any lightweight, sandable joint compound. No nails are used and joints with gaps up to ⅛ inch easily are filled with the same joint compound used to install the molding. Also, inside miter joints are used instead of coped joints. Cut the molding with a miter box or chop saw and use the same paint you use on the walls.

1 Cut the molding as you would wood molding, except make miter cuts instead of copes for inside corners. Use a putty knife to apply a ⅜-inch-wide swath of lightweight sandable joint compound to the top and bottom edges of the crown.

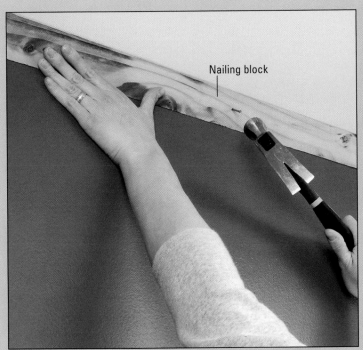

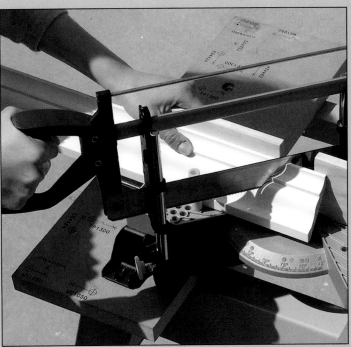

3 If the wall runs parallel to the ceiling joists, there may be no framing members in position to nail the molding to the ceiling. In this situation, cut some triangular nailing blocks to attach to the wall studs. Size the blocks to allow a ¼-inch gap between the block and the back of the crown.

4 The second piece of crown is cut square on one end and coped on the other. To cut the cope, start with an inside miter cut. Hold the crown in your miter box upside down (as if the base of the box were the ceiling, and the fence were the wall) and backwards (if the cope is on the right end of the piece, the cut will be on the left as the piece rests in the miter box).

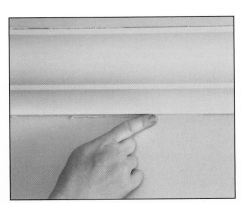

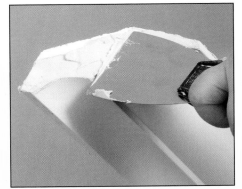

2 Press the molding into place causing the joint compound to ooze out along the length. Use your finger to smooth the excess where the molding meets the ceiling and wall.

3 To join two pieces in a straight run, use a butt joint. Wherever one piece of molding joins another, coat the adjoining face of the second piece with joint compound before you press it into place. Wipe off the excess squeeze-out with a damp sponge.

4 After the adhesive dries, smooth joints with a fine-grit sanding sponge. The sponge will conform to the shape of the molding. Dab in joint compound to fill any gaps and sand again as needed.

Installing crown molding (continued)

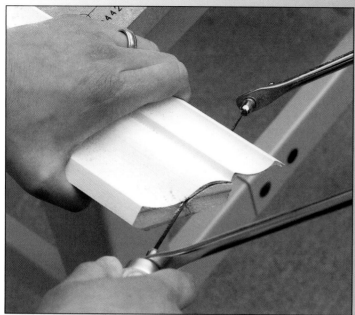

5 Create the cope by sawing along the intersection of the miter cut and the face of the profile. Angle the saw slightly so the joint is undercut. Test the fit against a piece of scrap molding and fine-tune the piece with a utility knife. Nail the piece in place as before. Proceed around the room, making square cuts on one end, coped cuts on the other end of each piece. Make coped cuts on both ends of the last piece.

6 For outside miters, the pieces also are held in the saw upside down and backwards, but the cut is angled in the opposite direction. To get a tighter fit in both outside and inside corners, you can flex and twist the pieces slightly before driving in the nails closest to the joint.

WHAT IF ...
You need to end crown molding without running into a wall?

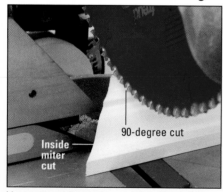

90-degree cut

Inside miter cut

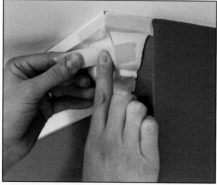

You may need to end a run of crown molding that doesn't turn a corner or run into a wall. If so, stop the molding with a triangular return piece that carries the profile to the wall. To cut this piece, place a scrap of crown upside down in the chop saw or miter box and make an outside miter cut. Then set the saw to 90 degrees, cut off the triangle, aligning the blade to the point where the miter ends at the back of the molding. Attach the return piece with yellow carpenter's glue. Use masking tape to hold the piece in place until the glue sets.

STANLEY PRO TIP

Burnish corners to cure gaps

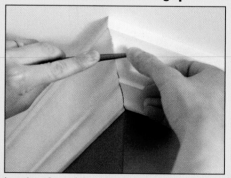

In spite of careful work, not every joint will fit perfectly. If you find a slight gap in an outside miter, force a little glue into it, then burnish the edges using the side of a nail set. Burnishing the corners folds over the thin wood fibers, bridging the gap.

INSTALLING CHAIR RAIL AND PICTURE FRAME MOLDING

Along with baseboard and crown, you'll find two other moldings typically installed on walls: chair rail and picture frame molding. Chair rail is installed about 34 to 36 inches above the floor. It helps break up the vertical surface of a wall and protects the wall from damage from chair backs or other furniture.

Picture frame molding, installed around a room about 18 inches down from the ceiling, also breaks up the vertical expanse of a wall. Its practical function is to serve as a ledge from which to hang pictures. Rather than scar a wall with nails or screws, you hook a stiff wire (or wires) over the molding, extend it down the wall, and attach it to the back of the frame.

Both types of molding are installed similarly to crown and baseboard, using coped joints for inside corners and miter joints for outside corners.

Chair rail: Some molding is sold specifically as chair rail, but you can make your own by combining moldings. Here a piece of cap molding is added to an inverted piece of baseboard to create a wide chair rail.

Picture frame molding: In a room with standard 8-foot ceilings, a full complement of molding (base, chair, picture, and crown) is overkill. If you like picture frame molding, consider applying it to one or two walls only.

Solo measuring

Making a measurement along a wall from one side of a room to the other can be a real challenge if you are working alone. Because walls sometimes lean in or out, you want to get the measurement right at the height where your molding will run. It can be difficult to hold your tape measure in exactly the right place.

To make things easier, drive a nail into a stud near one side of the room where the hole will be covered by the molding. Measure from the corner to the nail. Then hook your tape on the nail and measure to the other corner. The sum of these two measurements is the number you're looking for.

Staying on the level

The trick to installing chair rail is to keep it level. Rather than bothering with chalk lines or levels, cut a spacer from a piece of scrap and use it to hold the molding at a constant height above the floor. This works well as long as the floor is reasonably level.

INSTALLING WAINSCOTING

A traditional wall treatment that lends a quiet air of quality and warmth to a room, wainscot paneling also makes an extremely durable wall, because wood is much more resilient than drywall.

Wainscoting includes any type of wooden paneling applied to the bottom half of a wall. The tongue-and-groove, beaded-board wainscoting in this project is among the most popular styles. Beaded board is available in various widths and in thicknesses from ¼ inch to ¾ inch. This project uses ¼-inch-thick boards under ½-inch-thick baseboard to match the thickness of ¾-inch-thick door and window casing.

PRESTART CHECKLIST

☐ **TIME**
About 6 hours for an 8-foot section of wainscoting

☐ **TOOLS**
Tape measure, chalk line, chop saw or miter box, hammer, nail set, circular saw or saber saw, block plane

☐ **SKILLS**
Measuring and laying out, crosscutting, driving finish nails

☐ **PREP**
Empty room of all furnishings

☐ **MATERIALS**
¼-inch-thick beaded tongue and groove, ½-inch×4-inch baseboard, cap molding, 8d finish nails, 4d finishing nails

Use a 1-foot scrap of tongue-and-groove board to help snug boards without damaging the groove. Put the tongue of the scrap into the groove of the piece you are installing. Then tap on the tongue side of the scrap with your hammer.

1 This project uses a ½-inch-thick cap rail. Snap a chalk line ½ inch below the height you select for the cap rail. Cut ¼-inch-thick beaded tongue-and-groove boards to ¼ inch shorter than the line.

2 Apply a bead of construction adhesive to the back of each board. Insert the tongue of each board into the groove of the board before. Position the tops along the chalk line and leave a gap at the floor.

WHAT IF ...
You have to turn an outside corner?

1 If your wainscoting wraps around an outside corner, put the last piece in place without adhesive. Use a sharp pencil to scribe the location of the corner along the back of the piece. Using a circular saw or saber saw, cut to the pencil line but don't cut away the line. The idea is to allow the last piece to extend very slightly past the corner, thereby creating a tight joint with the next piece.

2 Use a block plane to remove the tongue from the piece that turns the corner. Put construction adhesive on the piece and attach it with the planed face flush to the face of the adjacent piece.

3 Use a box extender to move electrical outlet and switch boxes out ¼ inch. **Turn off power to the room at the circuit box.** Disconnect the receptacle or switch. Use a saber saw to cut boards to fit around the box. Insert a box extender. Reconnect the switch or receptacle and replace the cover plate before turning the power back on.

4 Put the second-to-last piece before a corner in place without adhesive. Measure from the base of the tongue to the wall at top and bottom. If the measurements differ, transfer them to the top and bottom of the last piece to lay out a tapered cut. Make the cut with a saber saw.

5 Because of the tongue, the last two pieces at a corner must be snapped in place together. Put adhesive on the wall. Fit the last two pieces together. Bend them in a bit at the joint and fit the second-to-last tongue into place. Press at the joint to snap the last two pieces into place. Use a block plane to remove the tongue of the first board that turns the corner.

6 Before installing the first piece that turns an inside corner, use a block plane to shave the tongue off the piece. Install the piece with the shaved side in the corner.

7 Attach ½-inch×4-inch baseboard over the bottom of the wainscoting with two 8d finishing nails into each stud.

8 Attach a cap molding along the top of the wainscot to cover the top edge of the paneling. Use yellow carpenter's glue and 4d nails driven at a slight angle toward the wall to ensure they don't come through the face of the top molding.

Cap molding

GLOSSARY

Apex: The uppermost point, also the point of an angle.

Apron: The bottom piece of window casing that finishes the window frame beneath the sill (stool).

Baseboard: Trim running along the bottom of a wall to cover gaps between the wall and floor and to protect the bottom of the wall. (See also Base shoe and Cap molding)

Base cap: A piece of molding that covers the top of the traditional baseboard.

Base shoe: A narrow, flexible piece of molding that covers the joint between baseboard and floor. Sometimes called shoe molding.

Bearing wall: A wall that carries a portion of the weight of the building above it.

Bifold door: A door that folds in half as it opens. Often used in pairs as closet doors.

Blocking: Pieces of lumber that are nailed horizontally between wall studs to serve as anchor points for molding or cabinetry. Blocking is also installed between floor joists to stiffen the floor or to provide a nailing surface for the top of a partition wall.

Bow: A defect in which a board is warped along its length when viewed along its narrow dimension.

Butt joint: A joint where ends of the two adjoining pieces are cut square and the pieces are simply placed against each other. The pieces can be butted end to end if you need to extend a piece of molding. Or, if you are turning a corner, the end of one piece butts into the side of the other.

Bypass doors: Doors that open by sliding past each other—often used for closets. The main advantage of bypass doors is that they need no swing room to open. The disadvantage is that only one-half the opening is accessible at a time.

Cap molding: A molding made to be applied to the top edge of another material as a finishing treatment.

Casing: Trim that surrounds a door or window opening.

Chair rail: Trim running across a wall approximately midway between the ceiling and the floor. Though often used for decorative purposes, chair rail is designed to protect the wall from chairs, particularly in dining rooms.

Check: A crack in a board.

Circuit breaker: A protective device in a service panel that automatically shuts off power to its circuit when it senses a short or circuit overload.

Coped joint: A joint between two pieces of molding where the end of one piece is cut to accommodate the profile of the other. Usually used for inside corners.

Coping saw: A saw with a thin blade held in a C-shape frame. A coping saw readily cuts curves and is most often used for making coped joints.

Corner bead: A plastic or metal molding that is attached to outside drywall corners to make them easier to finish and to protect them from damage.

Cripple stud: A short stud. Most typically used above door openings in nonbearing walls and below window openings.

Crook: A defect in a board in which the board is warped along its length when viewed along its wide dimension.

Cross cut: To cut a board across its width to make it the right length.

Crown molding: One type of molding installed where wall meets ceiling.

Cup: A defect in a board where the board is warped across its width.

Dado: A flat-bottomed groove cut across a board.

Deadman: A T-shape brace used to help hold drywall in place against ceiling joists while drywall is fastened in place.

Dimension lumber: Lumber that is 2 to 5 inches in nominal thickness and up to 12 inches in nominal width.

Door strike: The metal hardware attached to the doorframe that receives the bolt from the lockset. Also called a strike plate.

Drywall: A sheet product made for use as a wall surface, consisting of paper faces covering a core of gypsum.

Fire stop: A piece of wood nailed across a stud bay to prevent the bay from acting as a chimney and conduit for fire.

Framing: The structure of the house. This term encompasses all the wooden parts of a house's frame including the wall studs, headers, joists, rafters, etc.

Furring strips: Strips of wood attached to a surface as spacers/anchor points for an additional wall surface. Basement walls often have furring strips added to provide a place to attach drywall. Often made from 1×2s or 1×3s.

Header: The part of a house's frame that spans a door or window opening. Often made from two pieces of 2× lumber with a spacer of ½-inch plywood. Also, any piece of wood (such as trim) which spans the top of an opening.

Hinge mortise: The recessed areas cut in the edge of a door and its frame to accommodate the hinge leaves.

J-bead: A molding made to cover the edge of a drywall sheet so the raw edge does not show in the finished product.

Jack stud: One part of the pairs of studs that make up a door or window opening. The jack studs are cut to match the height of the opening. The header for the opening rests on top of the jack studs. Sometimes called a trimmer. (See also King stud)

Jamb: The wooden frame that lines a door or window opening.

Joist: A horizontal part of a house's frame that carries floor and/or ceiling.

King stud: One part of the pairs of studs that make up a door or window opening. The king studs are cut to the same length as the other wall studs. The jack studs are nailed to the king studs.

Lath: Thin strips of wood that are applied to a wall surface to serve as a substrate for plaster. More recent plasterwork often uses an expanded metal mesh as lath.

Lauan: A tropical hardwood that is often cut into veneers to cover hollow core doors and plywood. Sometimes called Philippine mahogany.

Level: Perfectly horizontal with no part higher or lower than another. Also, a tool used to measure this condition.

Lockset: The hardware used for keeping a door closed, usually consisting of doorknobs, lock, bolt, and strike plate.

Miter: A corner joint between two pieces of wood where the adjoining ends are cut at matching angles. Also, the process of cutting these angles.

Mud: In the construction business, any of a number of wet materials which harden when they dry (such as mortar). In interior work, mud usually refers to the joint compound used to fill the nail holes and seams in drywall.

Nail pops: Places in finished drywall where a nail has begun to back out of the stud (or was never completely driven home). Nail pops show up as a small circular lump on the wall surface.

Partition wall: A wall whose only purpose is to divide a space—it does not contribute to supporting the weight of the building.

Penny: Commonly used term for describing the length of nails, abbreviated as "d." The higher the penny number, the longer the nail.

Picture frame molding: A decorative molding applied around the walls of a room approximately 18 inches from the ceiling. Designed to accept hooks for hanging framed pictures without putting nail holes in a wall.

Plate: A horizontal piece of lumber to which the wall studs are attached. The bottom plate is anchored to the floor. The top plate is usually a double thickness to tie walls together and help carry the load from above.

Plumb: Perfectly vertical. This can be measured using a level or a plumb bob.

Plywood: A sheet product made from thin layers of wood (veneers) glued in a sandwich. Generally available in 4×8 sheets.

Precuts: Studs purchased already cut to the right length for an 8-foot ceiling (92⅝ inches) allowing for a single bottom plate and a double top plate.

Prehung door: A door that is purchased already hinged and hanging within a complete door jamb.

Return: When used with regard to trim, a piece of molding which completes a run by turning into the wall.

Reveal: A narrow flat area on a molding or board left uncovered for visual effect.

Rip: To cut a board along its length. One rips a board to the needed width. Rip cuts are most easily accomplished with a table saw.

Roughing in: The process of installing the first stages of utilities such as plumbing and electrical wiring. This usually involves running the pipes and wiring that will be hidden inside the walls. The finish work (installing the various fixtures) is done after the walls are in place.

Rough opening: The opening in the framing made to accommodate a door or window.

Scarf joint: A joint used to extend the length of a board or piece of trim. Usually the pieces are cut with mating angles to help disguise the juncture.

Snapping a line: A term used to describe the process of marking a layout line with a chalk line. The chalk line is held taut between two points and plucked so it snaps against the surface. This action transfers chalk from the line to the surface.

Stool: A horizontal piece of trim installed at the bottom of a window, often called the sill.

Stop: A narrow strip of wood installed inside a door jamb which keeps the door from swinging too far closed.

Stud: The vertical members of a house's frame. Often made from 2×4s or 2×6s.

Stud bay: The space between two studs installed in a wall.

Subfloor: The first decking applied on top of the floor joists. Usually made from plywood. The finished floor, such as hardwood strips or carpet, is attached to the subfloor.

Toenailing: Driving a nail at an angle through one framing member so it can penetrate a second framing surface.

Twist: A defect in a board in which the board is warped along its length similar to an airplane propeller.

Warp: A surface that is not true or flat. Warp is any combination of bow, crook, cup, and/or twist.

Wainscoting: Wooden paneling applied to a wall. Traditionally wainscoting was made up of a series of frame and panel units, though today the term is used to describe almost any wooden paneling, particularly that which only reaches partway up a wall.

INDEX

METRIC CONVERSIONS

U.S. Units to Metric Equivalents			Metric Units to U.S. Equivalents		
To convert from	Multiply by	To get	To convert from	Multiply by	To get
Inches	25.4	Millimeters	Millimeters	0.0394	Inches
Inches	2.54	Centimeters	Centimeters	0.3937	Inches
Feet	30.48	Centimeters	Centimeters	0.0328	Feet
Feet	0.3048	Meters	Meters	3.2808	Feet
Yards	0.9144	Meters	Meters	1.0936	Yards
Square inches	6.4516	Square centimeters	Square centimeters	0.1550	Square inches
Square feet	0.0929	Square meters	Square meters	10.764	Square feet
Square yards	0.8361	Square meters	Square meters	1.1960	Square yards
Acres	0.4047	Hectares	Hectares	2.4711	Acres
Cubic inches	16.387	Cubic centimeters	Cubic centimeters	0.0610	Cubic inches
Cubic feet	0.0283	Cubic meters	Cubic meters	35.315	Cubic feet
Cubic feet	28.316	Liters	Liters	0.0353	Cubic feet
Cubic yards	0.7646	Cubic meters	Cubic meters	1.308	Cubic yards
Cubic yards	764.55	Liters	Liters	0.0013	Cubic yards

To convert from degrees Fahrenheit (F) to degrees Celsius (C), first subtract 32, then multiply by ⁵⁄₉.

To convert from degrees Celsius to degrees Fahrenheit, multiply by ⁹⁄₅, then add 32.